TEN MINUTES TO CURTAIN!

A COLLECTION OF

SHORT PLAYS

for the

YOUNG ACTOR

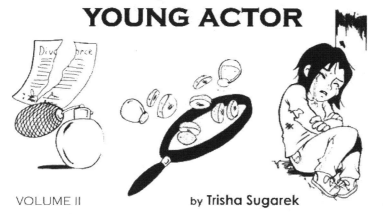

VOLUME II

by **Trisha Sugarek**

NOTICE

Illustrations by Angela Corbin

Made in the U.S.A.
All rights reserved.
ISBN#   978-1461119197

Table of Contents

.

Also by
TRISHA SUGAREK

…more by Trisha Sugarek

Fiction
Women Outside the Walls
Wild Violets
Song of the Yukon
Sisters

Children's Fiction
Stanley the Stalwart Dragon
The Exciting Exploits of an Effervescent Elf
Bertie, the Bookworm and the Bully Boys
Emma and the Lost Unicorn

Poetry
Butterflies and Bullets
The World of Haiku" with Sumi-E Artwork
Haiku Journal" -- a companion book
Moths and Machetes

Available at:
www.samuelfrench.com
www.writeratplay.com
www.amazon.com

PAN OF POTATOES

by

Trisha Sugarek

CAST OF CHARACTERS

Mama - the gentle matriarch of thirteen children.

Ivah - fifteen, the tomboy and prankster.

Violet - fourteen and a budding beauty.

Lillas - seventeen and the 'big' sister.

LaVerne - twelve and the baby of the family.

Scene 1

Setting. The Guyer farmhouse. 1920. The kitchen. Mid-morning.

*[The four Guyer **SISTERS** are setting the table, preparing breakfast and tea. **MAMA** is by the door putting on **HER** hat and coat.]*

MAMA. Violet, don't let that mush burn. And save enough tea leaves for our supper tonight.
VIOLET. Yes, Mama.
MAMA. Ivah, you and LaVerne be sure to get your chores done while I'm in town. Lillas is in charge while I'm gone.

*[The **GIRLS** begin to talk and squabble.]*

MAMA. *[In a quiet voice.]* And girls....

*[**THEY** don't hear her with all the noise **THEY** are making.]*

MAMA. GIRLS! *I'*m going into town and see Mr. Levine. Ask him for a little more credit until your father gets paid for that last load of lumber. I don't think that he'll let me shop on credit until the bill is paid down some but one can always hope. In the meantime, I've fried up the last of the bacon, onion and spuds in the iron skillet. That's supper.

*[The **GIRLS** groan.]*

MAMA. I know. But, that's all there is until your father gets back tomorrow. *[Laughs.]* We'll pretend we live in a shoe, have so many children we don't know what to do.
IVAH. But, Mama, I'm so hungry!
MAMA. There's plenty of mush and...
LAVERNE. Mama, if the hens have produced can we have an egg this morning?
MAMA. Yes, of course. But I don't expect you to find anything. They should be about finished with molting. Hopefully we'll be seeing some eggs in a couple of days.
LAVERNE. *Yes,* Ma'am.
 LILLAS. That's okay, squirt. I'll help you look.
MAMA. Now, while I'm gone, you get your chores done, clean up the breakfast dishes, then you can play a game here at the table until I get back. Violet, is your bed made?

VIOLET. Yes...*[Simultaneously.]*

IVAH. Is not.

VIOLET. Tattletale!

IVAH. Beast!

MAMA. Girls!

IVAH. She started it!

MAMA. What about the rest of you girls?

IVAH. *[Smirking.]* Yes, Ma'am, all done.

MAMA. Vi, get upstairs and make your bed. And be good, all of you!

      *[**SHE** exits.]*

VIOLET. You've got a big mouth, you know that?

IVAH. You shouldn't lie to Mama.

VIOLET. It was a little white lie; Mama says that's okay.

IVAH. Did not.

VIOLET. Did too.

      *[As lights dim **THEY** continue to squabble.]*

Scene   2

Setting. Four hours later. The kitchen.

> [**ALL** *the girls are sitting around the table playing Monopoly.* **IVAH** *is sitting in a chair closest to the stove.*]

VIOLET. A hotel on Park Avenue. I'm winning!

LILLAS. Don't count your chickens, Vi, 'til they're hatched.

LAVERNE. [*Grumbling.*] Darn old hens, anyway! Why do they have to be molting right when we haven't any food in the house? And what is 'molting' anyway?

> [**LILLAS** *throws the dice.*]

LILLAS. Damn! Jail, do not collect two hundred dollars.

LAVERNE. Swear word. I'm telllin' Mama.

LILLAS. No, you're not.

LAVERNE. Okay. What's molting, anyway.

VIOLET. They shed their feathers.

> [**THEY** *continue to play; meanwhile,* **IVAH** *is sneaking* **HER** *hand back into the pan of potatoes.*]

LAVERNE. Ugh! Then they're naked? Don't they get cold?

IVAH. Don't you know anything?   Yes! They're naked and they're so ugly your eye balls fall out.

LAVERNE. Really?

LILLAS. She's kidding you, squirt. They lose their old feathers and as soon as one is gone they start to grow a new one. But, it takes so much energy to do all that, they don't lay eggs.

> [**THEY** *continue to play and* **IVAH** *continues to sneak bites of the potatoes.*]

VIOLET. LaVerne, pay attention! You landed on Boardwalk. You wanna buy a hotel or something?

LAVERNE. Lillas? What should I do? I don't have much money.

LILLAS. Go for it!

IVAH. *[Talking with her mouth full.]* Yeah, buy a bootel…

VIOLET. Ivah, what are you eating?

IVAH. Nothing.

VIOLET. You are! What is it? I want some.

> [**LILLAS** *looks from* **IVAH***'s guilty face to the pan on the stove.*]

LILLAS. Ivah! You've been eating our supper?

> [**LILLAS** *gets up and crosses to the stove.*]

You have! You've eaten almost all of the potatoes.

IVAH. Well, so what. I'm hungry!

VIOLET. But Mama said that's all we have.

IVAH. Oh, Fiddleydee! She'll get some credit and bring back supper fixin's.

VIOLET. What a selfish pig!

IVAH. Oh, shut up!

LAVERNE. You said, 'shut up'. Ivah, I'm telling.

IVAH. You shut up!

LILLAS. What are we going to tell Mama?

IVAH. NOTHING! You know our code, 'one for all and all for one'. You can't snitch me out.

Scene   3

Setting. The Kitchen. An hour later.

[MAMA enters. SHE takes HER coat and hat off. HER hands are empty. The GIRLS all sit at the table, silent.]

MAMA. Hello, girls. Sorry I was so long. That old skinflint, Levine, refused me credit. Told me my bill was too high and to 'bring him some money, then the store was mine'. Old badger. *[Silence.]* Well, never mind. It's bacon and spuds for us. Thank goodness we have that. Put your game away now and set the table.

[Silence. MAMA looks at THEM.]

What's happened? Who did what?
LILLAS. There's no bacon and spuds, Mama.

[MAMA crosses to the stove.]

MAMA. Of course there is. I fried them up this morning before I left. Plenty for everybody....*[She looks into the pan. She turns.]*....Alright, what happened to supper? These potatoes didn't just sprout feet and run away.

[Silence. The GIRLS look at each other and then glare at IVAH.]

Oh, I see. 'One for all and all for one' is it?

[The GIRLS all stare at MAMA in shock.]

You thought I didn't know about your code of honor? *[Beat.]* You think anything in this house gets past your Mama? *[Silence.]* Well? I asked you girls a question. Are you going to tell me who did this? *[Silence.]*Well! That's fine. Humph! 'One for all,' is it? Well, good then *all* of you will be punished equally. Until the guilty party confesses to this greed, none of you are allowed to call me 'Mama'.

LAVERNE. But, Mama....

LILLAS. Mama....

[The **GIRLS** *murmur with horror.* **MAMA** *hold up* **HER** *hand to silence* **THEM.***]*

MAMA. And, you two, your punishment for calling me 'Mama' will be to clean out the chicken coop tomorrow morning. I don't want to hear another word until the person who did this comes to me. Now, get on up to bed without supper.

VIOLET. But, Mama, it's not even dark yet....

MAMA. One week of doing dishes for you young lady.

[As **THEY** *exit,* **THEY** *mutter to each other under* **THEIR** *breath.]*

IVAH. Meeting at the outhouse.

VIOLET. *[Angry.]* Why should we?

LILLAS. Because we need to figure this out.

*[***THEY** *exit. The* **GIRLS** *re-enter far down stage.]*

LAVERNE. I hate the outhouse. It stinks.

VIOLET. Hush up..... Mama will hear us.

IVAH. Hold your nose.

LILLAS. Is that what you did while you ate our supper?

IVAH. Be quiet. I didn't know I had eaten so much. I thought I took just a couple of bites.

LILLAS. Well, you didn't. And now all of us are in trouble. I have never, in my life, been forbidden to call Mama, 'Mama'.

LAVERNE. I don't like this punishment. I want to call Mama by her name.

VIOLET. Ivah, you've got to tell Mama. This isn't fair. It's a terrible punishment. I'd rather cut my own switch and be licked with it than this.

IVAH. She's gonna be so mad at me. I can't tell her.

LILLAS. You've got to. It's not right that we are being punished when we didn't do anything wrong.

IVAH. I can't. Mama called the person who did this 'greedy'.

LILLAS. Yes, and that person is you!

VIOLET. I for one are not going to speak to you, loan you my hair ribbons, go places with you, or kill spiders for you, UNTIL YOU TELL MAMA THE TRUTH!
LAVERNE. Me too!
LILLAS. We have to vote. One for all and ...
IVAH. Yeah, yeah, we know, Lillas. Give it a rest.
LILLAS. *[Ignoring Ivah.]A*ll in favor of ignoring Ivah until she tells Mama, say 'Ay'.
VIOLET. 'Ay'.
LAVERNE. 'Ay'.
 LILLAS. 'Ay'. 'Nays?'
IVAH. Nay.
VIOLET. Your vote doesn't count.
IVAH. This isn't fair.

> *[The* **GIRLS** *stare at* **HER***.* **THEY** *have begun ignoring* **HER***.]*

Can't we talk about this?

> *[Silence. The* **GIRLS** *turn and leave* **IVAH** *alone.* **THEY** *exit.]*

Scene   4

Setting. Several days later. The kitchen.

[IVAH sits at the table alone doing homework. MAMA is at the sink.]

IVAH. Mama.....I mean, Mrs. Guyer.
MAMA. I'll let that slide, Ivah. What is it?
IVAH. I can't stand this. It's been almost a week and none of the girls will talk to me, Lillas and LaVerne wouldn't even let me help them clean out the chicken coop. Violet won't do anything with me.
MAMA. So....you're ready to tell me the truth?
[IVAH looks at HER mother in shock.]
IVAH. You knew? All this time, you knew!
MAMA. I know my girls. It was a pretty good guess who ate our supper.
IVAH. But, if you knew, why didn't you just say?
MAMA. Because then none of you would have learned anything.

[IVAH rises and rushes to MAMA.]

IVAH. Mama, I'm so sorry. I really didn't mean to eat the supper. I was sneaking a few bites and then suddenly it was mostly gone. Please, please forgive me. Please don't think I'm greedy.....*[She begins to cry.]* even though it looks like I am. I'm so very sorry.
MAMA. Now, now. It's not the end of the world. Dry your tears. Did you learn anything, Ivah?
IVAH. Yes, Ma'am. Not to eat potatoes.

*[**MAMA** can't help but laugh.]*

MAMA. Yes, that too. But, I hope you also learned that you have to think of others sometimes. You can't be selfish. And above all else you must tell the truth and own up to your mistakes. Because no matter what you might do, I will always, always love you.

IVAH. Yes, Mama. *[Beat.] W*hat's my punishment going to be?

MAMA. I think you've been punished enough. Now, be a good girl, go out and get me a few carrots from the garden.

CURTAIN

The Straight-edged Secret

by

Trisha Sugarek

CAST OF CHARACTERS

Adriana - A teenager

Brian - Adriana's eleven year old step-brother

Jacquelyn - Adriana's mother

Cameron - Adriana's step-father

Mrs. Marzano - the Therapist

Note: 'For most cutting is an attempt to interrupt strong emotions and pressures that seem impossible to tolerate. It can be related to broader emotional issues that need attention. Most of the time, cutting is not a suicide attempt.

Cutting affects many teens and preteens — even beyond those who self-injure. Many teens worry about a friend who cuts, or face pressure from peers to try cutting as a daring thing to do.

In many cases, cutting — and the emotions that go along with it — is something teens struggle with alone. But because of growing awareness, more teens can get the assistance they need.

Parents can help teens who cut — and the earlier, the better. Cutting can be habit-forming, and sadly, many people underestimate the risks of getting seriously sick or hurt that go along with it.'

Courtesy of: www.kidshealth.org/parent/emotions/behavior/help_cutting.html
Production notes:

Dinner does not have to be served during Scene 2. It can be replaced with another activity depending upon the director's needs.

Scene   1

Setting.   A stark white room, like a bathroom.

> *[ADRIANA sits on a chair. **SHE** is wearing shorts and a tank top. **SHE** holds a razor blade. **SHE** is cutting shallow cuts into **HER** thigh. Tears stream down her face.]*

ADRIANA. *[She sighs with relief.]* Oh, Gosh.

> *[A pounding on the door, **OFF**, the voice of a young boy.]*

VOICE OFF. Ad, open up! You've been hoggin' the bathroom for *hours*!

> *[As **ADRIANA** pats the bleeding cuts with tissues, **SHE** yells through the door.]*

ADRIANA. Shut up and get away from the door, Brian, if you know what's good for you.
VOICE OFF. I'm tellin' Mom.

ADRIANA. *[Yells back.]* Go ahead, you little beast. *[Murmurs.]* One more disappointment to tell Cameron about.

> *[**ADRIANA** holds the paper tight against the cuts. **SHE** rises and, with a towel, wipes her face. **SHE** stuffs the blood stained paper into her pocket. A soft knocking is heard at the door.]*

JACQUELYN. Addy? Are you almost finished? Brian needs to use the bathroom.
ADRIANA. Just a sec, Mom.

*[**JACQUELYN** calls to **HER** son.]*

JACQUELYN. Brian, Adriana is done, you can use the bathroom now. *[Beat.]* Brian!

*[Wiping **HER** tears with the bottom of HER top, **ADRIANA** reaches to unlock the door.]*

Scene 2

Setting. The dining room.

> *[ADRIANA and JACQUELYN are sitting at a dining room table. It is set for dinner. ADRIANA has a school book at HER place.]*

ADRIANA. Where's the brat tonight?

JACQUELYN. Addy, I wish you would not call your brother names.

ADRIANA. Mom, all my friends call their little brothers and sisters names. That's what we *do*! It doesn't mean anything.

JACQUELYN. *Brian* is still at baseball. He'll eat later.

ADRIANA. When's Cameron getting in?

JACQUELYN. He called from the airport about an hour ago. He should be here in a few minutes.

ADRIANA. Can we start dinner without him? I need to get on my homework.

JACQUELYN. Let's wait a few minutes. It's so rare that we get to have dinner with him during the week.

ADRIANA. *[Sighing.]* I don't see why it matters. He's just going to yell at me about the 'A minus' I got in physics.

JACQUELYN. Addy, be fair now. Cam does not 'yell' at you.

ADRIANA. He might as well. He uses a low, calm voice but it still feels like yelling to me.

JACQUELYN. He just wants you to do well, to succeed. He's very proud of you being on the honor roll year after year.

ADRIANA. Yeah, like the world would end if I wasn't on the honor roll. How would he explain that to his friends?

JACQUELYN. Adriana, that's not nice and isn't true....

> *[A door slams and CAMERON, Adriana's step-father calls from OFF.]*

CAMERON. Hey! Where is everyone? The bread winner is home from the wars!

ADRIANA. Jeeesch!

JACQUELYN. *[Laughing.]* We're in here, darling. Dinner's almost ready.

[CAMERON enters, crosses to JACQUELYN and kisses HER on the cheek. As HE passes ADRIANA, HE ruffles her hair.]

ADRIANA. *[Smoothing her hair.]* Hi, Cameron.
JACQUELYN. How was the flight, Sweetie?
CAMERON. Long and boring. What's for dinner?
JACQUELYN. Baked pork chops with veggies and apple pie for desert.
CAMERON. My favorite.*[Laughing.]* I should come home more.
ADRIANA. *[Whining.]* Moomm…you know I don't eat meat.
CAMERON. Addy, some respect, please. You'll eat what your mother….
JACQUELYN. It's okay, Cam. I made extra veggies, honey, and some pasta.
CAMERON. You spoil her, you know. *[Beat.]* Where's Brian?
JACQUELYN. Baseball practice. He'll be home in about an hour. I'll get dinner. Do you want a glass of wine?
CAMERON. That sounds great.

[JACQUELYN exits and CAMERON eases back in HIS chair, pulling his tie off.]

CAMERON. *[Indicating the text book.]* What're you working on?
ADRIANA. Physics.
CAMERON. Good girl.

[JACQUELYN enters with serving dishes and a glass of wine on a tray.]

JACQUELYN. Okay, dinner is served. Addy, put your homework aside please.

[Just then ADRIANA's cell phone buzzes. SHE grabs for it.]

CAMERON. Uh-uh. Don't answer it. No cell phones during dinner.
ADRIANA. *[Under her breath.]* It's a dumb rule.
CAMERON. *[HE picks up her cell phone.]* Maybe you'll think again about the cell phone rule if you don't have one.
JACQUELYN. Adriana, apologize to your Dad and turn off your phone, please.
ADRIANA. *[Making a point of using his name.]* Sorry, *Cameron.*
CAMERON. Dinner smells wonderful, Jackie.

[A few beats as dishes are passed and THEY begin to eat.]

JACQUELYN. I made you some pasta, Ad, be certain I see some of it on your plate. You can't live on vegetables alone.

ADRIANA. *[Reaches for food.]* Okay! Do you have to nag me morning *and* night?

CAMERON. That's enough, Adriana.

ADRIANA. Not quite. Go ahead, Mom, tell him about my grade in physics.

[**ADRIANA** *wants to needle* **CAMERON** *for taking* **HER** *phone.*]

JACQUELYN. Oh, honey, let's wait 'till after dinner. We have a nice meal here; let's enjoy it.

CAMERON. What about your grade in physics? You nailed it, right?

ADRIANA. Sorry to disappoint you *again*, Cameron, but I got an 'A minus' on my mid-term.

[**CAMERON** *throws* **HIS** *napkin on the table, in disgust.*]

CAMERON. What the hell happened? You sail through physics like it was Kindergarten's ABC's. Did you study? Or were you too busy texting your friends all night?

JACQUELYN. Cam, please.

ADRIANA. I missed a matter interaction question.
It was a trick question and I didn't realize it. One missed question and the dumb teacher gives me a minus.

CAMERON. You deserved it for not paying attention. Jeez, Adriana, you know better.

ADRIANA. Says you. He could have left it an 'A'…it was just one dumb question!

JACQUELYN. Hey, you two, it doesn't matter. She's still on the honor roll and *[Turning to Adriana.]* I'm sure you'll ace your final.

CAMERON. Not without some dedication on her part.

[**ADRIANA** *throws* **HER** *napkin into* **HER** *plate and pushes back* **HER** *chair.*]

ADRIANA. May I be excused? I've got a ton of homework.

JACQUELYN. Of course, dear.

CAMERON. Not until you help your mother clear the table.

JACQUELYN. That's alright, Cam….

CAMERON. No. It's not all right. The least Adriana can do is help you and load the dishwasher.

ADRIANA. *[Sarcastic.]* Okay! *Then* can I have my phone back? *[Beat.]* Oh by the way, *[wants to needle Cameron.]* this is Dad's weekend and I'm definitely going.

Scene   3

Setting. The bathroom.

[ADRIANA is sitting. SHE lifts the razor blade and scores HER leg. A bright red line of blood follows the blade. SHE sighs with relief and begins to cry.]

ADRIANA. *[To herself.]* Why can't I be perfect like everyone expects? Why can't I be the perfect daughter Cameron wants so badly? Why do I disappoint my teachers? Why don't I have more friends?

[As SHE asks the questions, SHE cuts again. Suddenly the door burst open and JACQUELYN walks in. ADRIANA grabs a towel and covers HER leg. JACQUELYN looks at ADRIANA's leg in horror and then at ADRIANA'S face and then back to her leg. THEY speak simultaneously.]

ADRIANA. *[Panicked.]* MOM!! Don't you knock? Get out!
JACQUELYN. Ad, you're bleeding! How did that happen?
ADRIANA. Get out!
JACQUELYN. *[Pulling away the towel.]* Let me see, honey.
ADRIANA. Stop! Get out!

[THEY have a brief tug-a-war with the towel. ADRIANA finally lets go and gives up. JACQUELYN finally sees the razor blade.]

JACQUELYN. Addy, oh honey, what have you done?

ADRIANA. I'm sorry, Mommy.

JACQUELYN. *[In shock, she doesn't know what to say.]* Honey, did you do this? What happened?

> *[JACQUELYN gathers ADRIANA into HER arms. SHE rocks HER.]*

JACQUELYN. My baby….what have you done?
ADRIANA. It's okay, Mom….it's okay.
JACQUELYN. But, baby, why are you hurting yourself?
ADRIANA. It doesn't hurt, Mom. It feels kinda good.
JACQUELYN. But, honey, why? *[Beat.]* Why?
ADRIANA. 'Cause I'm a failure. Everybody knows it. Cameron, my friends, my teachers, even you.
JACQUELYN. No, no, you're not a failure! Sweetie, how can you think that? We're so proud of you. You're so smart and pretty.

ADRIANA. Yeah, sure, ask Cameron how proud he is of his 'A minus' step-daughter.

> *[SHE sobs and hiccups all in the same breath.]*

 I keep disappointing him.
JACQUELYN. Oh, Addy, is that what this is all about. You think you are disappointing us?
ADRIANA. Well, aren't I? Cameron is always telling me I can do better. My teachers say the same thing. I'm trying, Mom, I really am.

> *[JACQUELYN moves ADRIANA away from HER just enough to look into her eyes.]*

JACQUELYN. Addy, baby, I want you to listen very carefully to me. *You are not disappointing me or your Dad or anyone!* I think you're amazing. We're going to make some changes, you hear me? *[Adriana nods.]* And *we*, you and I, are going to get some help with this…*[indicating the razor and leg.]* but until we do, I want you to promise me something. Will you?
ADRIANA. What?
JACQUELYN. Promise me that you won't hurt yourself again. Can you do that?
ADRIANA. I'll try, Mommy.
JACQUELYN. And this is my promise to you. If the pressure gets to be too much, you come to me and no matter what I am in the middle of; I will sit down with you so we can talk. Is it a deal?
ADRIANA. *[Very subdued.]* Yes.
JACQUELYN. *[Holding up her little finger.]* Pinky-swear?
ADRIANA. *[Hooking her little finger with her Mom's.]* Pinky-swear.

Scene 4

Setting. A therapist's office.

[The therapist, **MRS. MARZANO** *sits in a chair opposite* **ADRIANA**. **THEY** *are in the middle of the session.]*

MRS. MARZANO. Adriana**,** do you know what doctor, patient privilege is?
ADRIANA. Not exactly…no.
MRS. MARZANO. It means that no matter what you say to me, I won't tell a soul. Not your parents…no one.
ADRIANA. Oh.
MRS. MARZANO. Now, let's begin. Can you tell me how long you've been cutting yourself?
ADRIANA. Since about when I started high school.
MRS. MARZANO. Why do you think you're cutting yourself?
ADRIANA. *[Shrugs.]* I dunno.
MRS. MARZANO. *[A couple of beats of silence.]* Any thoughts at all?
ADRIANA. I dunno….it's feels good. I mean after the pain of the cut, it feels like….I dunno….relief?
MRS. MARZANO. Relief…that's a good word. Relief from what, do you think?
ADRIANA. Don't get me wrong, I love my step-Dad and my teachers are great. But, it just seems like everyone is always at me, ya know? *[Silence. Adriana is struggling to express herself. She shrugs again.]*
MRS. MARZANO. And can you tell me more about 'everyone always at you'? What does that mean to you?
ADRIANA. My teachers are always asking me what I want to do…. like in a career, you know? And what colleges am I going to apply to. And am I doing enough community service 'cause it

looks good on my applications. And stuff like, 'keep it up, Adriana, you don't want to mess up your honor roll ranking', on and on. And I'm never good enough for Cameron, my step-father. *[Silence again.]*

MRS. MARZANO. Tell me about him.

ADRIANA. He's okay. He's very successful in his job. He has to travel 'cause I guess he's high up in his company. My Mom seems to love him a lot. But, when he comes home he's like….I dunno….a second report card that I get. If I get any grade other than A-pluses he's on my case. He's constantly preaching about education and careers go hand-in-hand and all that stuff. He's never like that with Brian.

MRS. MARZANO. And who is Brian?

ADRIANA. He's my step-brother. He's eleven.

MRS. MARZANO. And why is Cameron different with his son?

ADRIANA. 'Cause he's a jock. Baseball and track. He doesn't even get very good grades and Cameron never gets on him about that. But, if Brian messes up when he's at bat, well, watch out!

MRS. MARZANO. So do you think Cameron treats you different?

ADRIANA. Duh…..Brian's got it really good. Hit the ball, get to first base and he's home free….no pun intended.

*[**MRS. MARZANO** smiles at how clever and smart **ADRIANA** is.]*

MRS. MARZANO. Do you think Cameron cares about you?

ADRIANA. I don't know. Sometimes I think he can't stand failure…and that's when I don't think he likes me, ya know? That if I fail at something, it reflects on him somehow.

MRS. MARZANO. Do *you* think failure, as you call it, is okay?

ADRIANA. I don't know. Failure has never been an option for me.

MRS. MARZANO. What does 'failure' look like?

ADRIANA. An 'A-minus'.

MRS. MARZANO. Do you think that doing your very best, even though you might fail, is acceptable?

ADRIANA. *[In a whisper.]* No.

*[**THEY** sit quietly for a few beats. **MRS. MARZANO** glances at the clock.]*

MRS. MARZANO. Our time's up for today, Adriana, but I'd like you to think about what you have told me here today. I'd like you to consider this; that after you have done your very best at something and it still doesn't work out, or as you said 'you've failed', that it's okay….that failure is okay because *you* know that you did your best. Will you think about that?

ADRIANA. *[With a glimmer of hope on her face.]* Yes, Mrs. Marzano, I will….think about that.

Scene   5

Setting. The therapist's office. A week later.

> *[The therapist,* **MRS. MARZANO** *sits in a chair opposite* **JACQUELYN** *and*
> **CAMERON**. **THEY** *are in the middle of a session without* **ADRIANA**.*]*

MRS. MARZANO. ……so, Adriana and I have been talking about pressure. Too much pressure from family, teachers, peers, brings low self-esteem. I think she understands now that she can't please everyone all of the time. She has to find her own level of achievement and set goals she can achieve and gain satisfaction from.

CAMERON. Well, I hope you're not looking at me when you talk about pressure. I only wanted what was best for the kid. Her mother tends to be a little lax.

MRS. MARZANO. It's not about blame, Cameron. It's about helping Adriana see that she also puts pressure on herself to achieve. Add that to the pressure from outside sources and something has to give. In Adriana's case, she is cutting herself to seek relief.

CAMERON. Well, I just don't get that! My God, she's got scars for heaven's sake! It's downright sick!

JACQUELYN. Cameron, please. That's why we're here. *[Beat.]* Mrs. Marzano, what can *we* do better?

MRS. MARZANO. We need to try to ease the pressure on your daughter. As parents, you need to evaluate the areas that you pressure her about.

CAMERON. So basically give her a free ride?

MRS. MARZANO. As I understand it, she's honor role, editor on her school paper, and is in sports. I am recommending that you curtail any further commitments in her schedule until we get this problem under control. And I recommend also that as parents you pick and choose what pressure you bring to bear on her. She seems to be succeeding in everything. So, no, Cameron, not a 'free ride'. Just let her succeed at what she is succeeding at right now and restrain yourself from any extra criticism.

JACQUELYN. That sounds like a good plan. We can do that, right, Cameron?

CAMERON. Sure, sure.

MRS. MARZANO. How's Brian? Does he have any questions? How much does he know about Adriana's cutting?

JACQUELYN. He knows that Adriana is not feeling well and that we are in counseling.

MRS. MARZANO. I would be happy to see him, with you present, of course, if you think…

CAMERON. Absolutely not! I don't want *my* son to get any ideas. He's fine just as he is.

MRS. MARZANO. Well, I just want you to know that sometimes it's helpful if the whole family is involved.

JACQUELYN. Has Adriana said she would like us all together for a meeting?

MRS. MARZANO. Not yet, but don't worry, Jacquelyn, she'll get there. For right now, she needs to know that she has a private place, just for her, where she can say anything she wants to and it will never leave this room. She's extremely bright.

CAMERON. What has she said about me? I suppose I'm the wicked step-father in all this.

MRS. MARZANO. Not at all. I think your approval is very, very important to her. That's why, Cameron, you must think about balancing your criticism and your praise. Can you try to do that?

CAMERON. Of course.

JACQUELYN. Mrs. Marzano, I would like to continue, as a family, for a while. Not just about Adriana's cutting but as a whole. Kind of a family health checkup.

CAMERON. Oh, come on, Jackie. I don't have time for that. We're doing okay.

JACQUELYN. *[Finally takes a stand.]* We obvious-ly aren't doing 'okay'. My daughter is cutting herself. I'm firm on this, Cam. This is deeper than just Adriana cutting herself. I think we all need a little help with our family dynamic.

MRS. MARZANO. Blended families such as yours do have special challenges.

JACQUELYN. I'm asking you to get behind this, Cam. You know if it was Brian I would do *anything* to help.

CAMERON. I know but…

MRS. MARZANO. Cameron, maybe I can help here. We would not need you here every week. We can stagger time with Jacquelyn and the kids and ask you to be in meetings every other week. How does that sound?

CAMERON. Yeah, okay, that should work.

[*JACQUELYN stares at* **HER** *husband intently.*]

I'll make it work!

JACQUELYN. Thank you, Cam.

MRS. MARZANO. Excellent. Our time's up for today but I'll see you back here in a week, Jacquelyn. I believe Adriana's appointment is Friday, right?

JACQUELYN. Yes, she's looking forward to it. She really likes you, Mrs. Marzano.

MRS. MARZANO. And Cameron, let's make you an appointment for week after next, all right?

Scene   6

Setting. The therapist's office. Two months later.

*[***MRS. MARZANO*** *sits in a chair opposite* **ADRIANA***.]*

MRS. MARZANO. So, Adriana, how'd your week go?

ADRIANA. Great, Mrs. M. I brought my physics grade up with my final so that 'A-minus' didn't do a thing to my grade point.

MRS. MARZANO. *[With a smile.]* Funny how things work out.

ADRIANA. You know that guy I told you about?

MRS. MARZANO. Chandler?

ADRIANA. He asked me to the freshman prom. Isn't that ridiculous?

MRS. MARZANO. *[Laughing.]* 'Ridiculous'. That's good, right?

ADRIANA. Yes, that's very good. Mom's taking me dress shopping.

MRS. MARZANO. That's wonderful Addy. And how are your exercises coming along? Any urge to cut?

ADRIANA. No Ma'am. Three weeks it's been now and no cutting. When the pressure starts to build in my chest, I do my exercises and talk to my Mom. Or my counselor at school; he's really sick. That would be 'cool' in your language. And since you suggested I write in a journal I've really enjoyed that. My Mom bought me a really pretty one.

MRS. MARZANO. And the websites; you're finding them helpful?

ADRIANA. Oh, yes. There are chat rooms and kids like me post their experiences for others to read. One kid writes poetry when he feels like he's going to cut. It makes me feel not so alone, you know?

MRS. MARZANO. That's very good, Addy. You're doing so well. I'm proud of you.

ADRIANA. Thanks, Mrs. M.

CURTAIN

THE **'D'** WORD

by

Trisha Sugarek

CAST OF CHARACTERS

Richard - the father.

Polly - the mother.

Josh - the son.

Sarah - the daughter.

Scene   1

Setting. The living room of Richard and Polly's home. Evening.

[RICHARD and POLLY sit as far away as THEY can from each other. JOSH enters. HE has an IPod and earplugs in HIS ears. HE looks at HIS parents and removes the earplugs.]

JOSH. Whas' up?
RICHARD. Sit down, son.
JOSH. I got homework.
POLLY. Sit down, Josh.

[JOSH begrudgingly crosses and sits.]

POLLY. Where's your sister?
JOSH. How should I know?
RICHARD. Hey! Watch that tone with your mother.
JOSH. *[Under his breath but still audible.]* Whatever...
POLLY. Josh, a little respect would be nice...

[SARAH's entrance interrupts POLLY.]

SARAH. Hi Daddy. You're home early. What's going on?

[SARAH crosses and sits next to HER father. RICHARD gives HER a hug.]

RICHARD. Hi Baby. Your mother and I thought it was time for a family meeting.

*[**JOSH** rolls **HIS** eyes.]*

JOSH. What'd I do now?
POLLY. Nothing. And please take the ear phones out and turn off your IPod.

*[With a sigh, **JOSH** complies. **SARAH** looks at her parents for several moments, frowning.]*

SARAH. What's wrong? Why are you two being so polite?
RICHARD. Kids, your mother and I want you to know that no matter what happens, we love you. But sometimes...

*[**SARAH** starts to cry and covers **HER** ears.]*

SARAH. No, no, no, I don't want to hear this.
POLLY. Sarah, honey, we need to talk to you both...
SARAH. NO! Daddy, please don't say it. Please,

Josh and I will do better; won't we Josh? Please don't leave.
JOSH. Sar', what the heck are you blubbering about?
RICHARD. Sarah, calm down. I have to leave... you yourself asked me why your mother and I fight so much. I'll see you a bunch, I promise.
JOSH. Yeah. Like you're ever home now.

*[Ignoring **JOSH**, he continues to **SARAH**.]*

RICHARD. Honey, don't cry. You'll hardly know I'm gone.
JOSH. So nothing new there.
 POLLY. Josh, you're not helping
JOSH. So what? Am I supposed to be happy you two are getting a divorce?
SARAH. *[Sobs.]*Divorce? Oh, no! Please, Daddy, don't. Please!
POLLY. Sarah, honey, let Daddy and I tell you kids what's going to happen. That way you won't be so scared.
JOSH. I'm not scared.
POLLY. Your father and I have not been happy for some time now...
 JOSH. *[Sarcastic.]* What else is new?
RICHARD. Josh, we need you to be respectful and a contributor. So cut the smart remarks.

POLLY. Anyway, as I was saying, your father and I think that a separation is a good idea. We're making everyone unhappy with all the arguments and harsh words.

SARAH. Please, please, can't you love each other? Can't you just get along?

RICHARD. It's not that easy, Princess. Sometimes adults, like your mother and I, still love each other but they're not in love anymore.

JOSH. *[Shoots a knowing look at Richard.]*
Or... they're in love with someone else now.

POLLY. That's enough, Josh.

SARAH. What's that supposed to mean? *[To her father.]* What's Josh talking about, Daddy?

RICHARD. Nothing, Baby. Josh doesn't know everything. In fact he knows shockingly little about life.

JOSH. *[Rises and exits.]* I am so outta here.

RICHARD. Josh! You come back here. *[A door slams.]*

SARAH. *[In a tiny voice.]* What's going to happen now?

RICHARD. Well, I'm going to move out and...

SARAH. NO! Daddy, please...

POLLY. Sarah, just hear us out.

RICHARD. I'm going to move out. I've got an apartment in town. Just fifteen minutes away. You can come there whenever you want. I've got a bedroom for you and Josh and...

SARAH. *[Crying.]* How can this be happening? Susan said to me the other day how I was lucky that my parents were so solid. She hates that her Mom and Dad are split up. How can I face her or my other friends?

[SARAH rises. SHE turns to HER mother.]

You did this! You're driving him away! I HATE YOU!

[SARAH rushes out of the room.]

RICHARD. Sarah!

POLLY. *[Sarcastic.]* Well! That went well.

RICHARD. And I suppose that's my fault too.

POLLY. If the shoe fits...

RICHARD. Geez, Pol, give it a rest.

POLLY. How's Mary?

RICHARD. I'm not having this discussion with you again. Leave Mary out of it.

POLLY. That's pretty hard to do when she's the one breaking up my family. *[Beat.]* Don't you see what you're doing to your children? Don't you care, Richard?

RICHARD. Of course, I care!

POLLY. Then don't do it, Rich...we can work through this. We can get counseling...

RICHARD. Stop! *[Softer.]* Just stop, will you? We've talked about all of this before. I'm sorry but it's too late.

[Silence.]

POLLY. Get out.

RICHARD. Pol...

POLLY. *[Angry.]* Get out, you selfish pig. How can you do this to your kids? Never mind about me. Don't you see how hurt and angry they are?

RICHARD. Of course I see...

   *[***POLLY*** stands.]*

 POLLY. Get out! Get out! Get out!

RICHARD. All right...I'm going...keep your voice down.

   *[***RICHARD*** rises and crosses the room.]*

 Tell the kids 'bye'. I'll talk to them tomorrow.

POLLY. GET OUT!

   *[***RICHARD*** exits. A car door slams **OFF**. ***POLLY*** sinks down onto the couch and buries her face in **HER** hands.]*

Scene 2

Setting. The next afternoon. The living room.

> [**POLLY** *is lying on the couch with a damp towel over* **HER** *eyes. The front door slams.* **JOSH** *walks into the living room.*]

POLLY. Don't slam the door, please Josh.
JOSH. Sorry, Mom. *[Beat.]* What's wrong? Are you sick?
POLLY. No, sweetie. Just a headache.
JOSH. Is there anything to eat? The lunch at school was gross.
POLLY. *[Smiling.]* The kitchen is down the hall on your right.
JOSH. Very funny. I'm gonna get a snack before I start my homework. What time's dinner?
POLLY. Same ol', same ol'. Six-thirty just like always.

> [**JOSH** *starts to exit.* **HE** *turns back.*]

JOSH. Hey! Is Sarah home yet?
POLLY. Not yet. Today's Wednesday. Cheer leading practice after school.
JOSH. Mom, she wasn't at school today.
POLLY. *[Sits up.]*What do you mean, not in school?
JOSH. Just what I said, she wasn't at school. At least, I didn't see her.
POLLY. Well, maybe you missed her.
JOSH. Much as I wish it wasn't true, I get to see her every day. Didn't today. It was kinda weird.
POLLY. Do you have your cell phone on you?

> [**JOSH** *nods and fishes it out of* **HIS** *pocket.*]

Call her for me.

[JOSH dials and listens.]

JOSH. Straight to voice mail.
POLLY. Are you certain you didn't see her, Josh?

[HE shakes HIS head. POLLY stays calm.]

Okay, buddy. She's probably in practice and turned her phone off. Go get your snack and start homework.
JOSH. Okay.

[Shrugging HE exits.]

Scene 3

Setting. The living room. Three hours later.

*[**POLLY** and **JOSH** sit on the couch. The front door slams. **RICHARD** rushes into the room.]*

RICHARD. Have you heard anything?

POLLY. No. I've called all her friends, nothing. The school confirmed that she was absent today.

RICHARD. What the devil happened? Why didn't the school call you and tell you she wasn't in school?

POLLY. School policy with honor roll kids is to call the parents on the second day of 'absent without a note'. They said they just assumed that she was out sick and I'd write her a note when she came back.

RICHARD. What'd she say to you this morning?

POLLY. I didn't see her before she left for school. She told me last night that she had an early committee meeting, before school, concerning the sophomore prom.

RICHARD. You didn't get up with the kids?

POLLY. I had a blinding headache and took something for it. I slept in.

RICHARD. Since when do my children get up and get themselves ready for school?

POLLY. Since over two years ago, Richard. They're not babies anymore. Oh, but wait! You're never at home to notice that they are teenagers now.

RICHARD. So my daughter skips school, disappears while my wife lays in bed with a headache.

POLLY. Don't make this my fault, Richard. I'm up every morning and more importantly, I'm here every evening. Can you say the same?

RICHARD. Give it a rest, Pol...

*[**JOSH** can't take it. **HE** interrupts.]*

JOSH. Mom! Dad! Enough! Can you both give it a rest so we can find Sar'?

RICHARD. He's right. *[Beat.]* Have you called her phone?

POLLY. *[Glares at him.]* Yes, of course you have. Have you called the police? I wanted to wait until you got here. I was certain she would walk in the door.

 RICHARD. I don't think we should wait. You call the police. I'll get in the car and start driving around. I've got my cell; call me if you hear anything.

> *[**RICHARD** rises and starts to exit.]*

JOSH. Dad, can I come with you? I know some places where she and her friends hang.

> [**RICHARD** *looks at* **POLLY** *who nods.]*

RICHARD. Sure, son. Be glad to have you with me.

> *[**THEY** exit. **POLLY** begins to dial **HER**   phone.]*

Scene   4

Setting. The living room. Two days later.

> [**RICHARD** *and* **POLLY** *sit together on the sofa.* **RICHARD** *is holding* **POLLY**'*s*
> *hand.*   **JOSH** *sits in a chair nearby.]*

POLLY. This has got to be a parent's worst nightmare. To see an 'Amber Alert' with *your* child's
name. My God, Richard, what if they don't find her? I can't stand it! I'll die.
RICHARD. Easy, Baby. They'll find her. It's going to be okay.
JOSH. *[Scared.]*Dad...

> [**POLLY'**s *cell phone rings.* **SHE** *grabs it off the coffee table.]*

POLLY. HELLO! Sarah, is that you?......Oh, Hello, Mrs. McClury. *[She covers the phone with her
hand.]*... It's Carolyn's mother. *[Back to the phone.]* I really can't talk now. I have to leave the
phone line open for Sarah….or the police. Yes. *[Listens for several beats.]* WHAT!? She's
there?...Oh, my God, she's there with you*?...[Listens, starts to cry with relief.]* Is she all right*?*
[Listens.] Yes, yes. Oh, thank you! Yes, we'll wait right here....Yes, I understand. No, no, that's
perfectly fine. *[Beat.]* Please, Mrs. McClury, will you tell her that she's not in trouble. Tell her to
just, please, come home. *[Listens.]* Yes, yes. See you in ten minutes. Thank you! Bye.
RICHARD. How long has she been at the McClury's?
POLLY. The whole time. Carolyn was hiding her in their basement. Mrs. McClury said she came
home early from work today and thought she heard water running. She went down in the basement
to see and found Sarah in the shower. She called us right away but not before she gave Sarah a good
talking to. She tried to apologize for that. *[She laughs with relief.]* It saves me from giving her a
lecture. Said she grounded Carolyn for a month.
JOSH. That's so lame. What's Sarah's punishment?
RICHARD. We'll decide later, Josh. When she gets here I want you to go to your room.

JOSH. Why?

RICHARD. Because I said so. First Mom and I need to talk to her alone. Then you can come back down. Deal?

JOSH. Whatever.

RICHARD. Thank you.

[The doorbell rings. **RICHARD** *and* **POLLY** *jump up. As* **THEY** *move to the door,* **JOSH** *exits.]*

POLLY. *[Off.]* Sarah! Baby, are you all right?

MRS. McCLURY. *[Off.]* I'm so sorry about this.

RICHARD. *[Off.]* Thanks, Mrs. McClury, Carolyn. Talk to you soon. Bye.

*[*ALL *three enter the living room.* **THEY** *sit on the sofa with* **SARAH** *between* **THEM**. **POLLY** *has* **HER** *arm around* **SARAH** *and* **RICHARD** *is holding* **SARAH***'s hand.]*

SARAH. Are you guys really mad at me?

RICHARD. No, Princess, we were just very worried.

POLLY. I'm not angry with you, Sar', but don't you ever scare me like that again.

SARAH. I'm sorry, Mom.

POLLY. What possessed you to run away like that?

SARAH. *[Crying.]* I couldn't stand it...Daddy's leaving...it hurts so much...

POLLY. Do you know what could have happened to you? Thank God Carolyn hid you in their basement. When I think what...

RICHARD. But nothing bad happened, Pol. Let's leave it at that.

SARAH. What's my punishment?

POLLY. Your Dad and I will let you know. *[Hugs Sarah.]* Tomorrow.

SARAH. Are you going to stay, Daddy?

RICHARD. Princess. I can't. Your running away didn't 'fix' anything. I know this is tough on you kids. I'm sorry about that. Your Mom and I love you so much and we're going to do everything possible to make this easier for you.

POLLY. Let me call Josh.

*[*POLLY *rises and exits.]*

POLLY *[Off.]* Josh. Come down, please. *[*POLLY *and* JOSH *enters the room and sit.]* Okay, family meeting. Richard, would you tell Josh what you were saying to Sarah.

RICHARD. Listen, buddy. I know that this is tough. And your Mom and I are really sorry that we're hurting you. We'll never stop loving both of you, you know that right? I'll still be your Dad even though I won't be living here. I'll see you anytime you want. **RICHARD.** You can come to my apartment whenever you want, right, Polly?

POLLY. Absolutely.

RICHARD. We'll have sleepovers.

JOSH. No way.

RICHARD. Order pizza with pineapple, and you can watch anything you want on TV for however long you want.

POLLY. I don't think we'll go quite that far. But, we'll see. The important thing to remember and know with all your heart is you two didn't do anything wrong. Your Dad and I screwed it up. And even though our living arrangements are going to change, it absolutely,   positively, does not change how much we love you.

RICHARD. Ditto for me.

SARAH. You're not going to leave us, like forever, right Daddy?

JOSH. Geez, Sar', you are so lame.

[**RICHARD** *looks hard at* **JOSH** *and turns to* **SARAH.**]

RICHARD. I would never leave you two guys. Your my kids, and ...[*hugs Sarah.*] You're my Princess. *[Beat.]* And, Josh...

JOSH. Yeah?

RICHARD. As the oldest, I expect you to watch over your sister and your Mom when I'm not here. Understand?

JOSH. Yeah, I guess.

RICHARD. And you both gotta promise to come and talk to one of us if you feel scared or worried. Got it, Josh?

JOSH. Got it, Dad.

RICHARD. Princess? You promise you'll come to one of us?

SARAH. I promise.

POLLY. Okay. Who wants hamburgers?

[*SARAH* and *JOSH* *jump up and exit.*]

Can you stay, Richard?

RICHARD. *[rising.]* For your hamburgers? Try to keep me away.

[**THEY** *exit,* **RICHARD** *puts a casual arm across* **POLLY**'s *shoulders.]*

CURTAIN

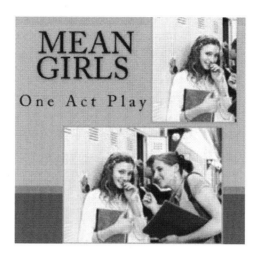

Mean Girls

by

Trisha Sugarek

CAST OF CHARACTERS

Bridgette - teenager

Jacquelyn - her mother

Gwen - a girl at school

Sue - a girl at school

Annie - a girl on the cheer squad

Scene   1

Setting. The school hallway. Mid-day. The second week of the school year.

(**GWEN** *and* **SUE** *stand together and watch* **BRIDGETTE** *walk toward* **THEM**.)

GWEN. *(Whispers.)* Here she comes now.
SUE. Look at her…she's so stuck up.
GWEN. Who does she think she is?
SUE. *(Sarcastic)* Big shot on campus…just because she was first draft at the cheerleading try-outs.
I heard she was on the competition team at her last school. Took state.
GWEN. That's just a rumor. I personally don't think she's all that good.

(**BRIDGETTE** *has gotten close enough to the girls to smile.* **HER** *smile dies when* **SHE**
realizes that **THEY** *are talking about* **HER**. **SHE** *averts her head and walks on by. The*
GIRLS *whisper just loud enough to be heard.*)

SUE. Ice Queen!
GWEN. Like, *so* cold. The blonde ice berg.
SUE. Look at her….she thinks she's all that.
GWEN. So stuck up, I can't believe it. She's not even pretty.
SUE. You know, Debbie lost her spot on the team because of that *(aims the word at Bridgette)* beee-
ach!
GWEN. *(Slightly shocked.)* Sue!
SUE. Well, she did. And Debbie's my friend and I don't appreciate someone, nobody even knows,
ruining Debbie's chances to cheer this year.

*(***BRIDGETTE*** *continues past and at a fast walk exits. The ***GIRLS****' voices follow ***HER****.)*

GWEN. She's got no friends.

SUE. Well, duh, she's stuck up. Doesn't talk to anyone.

GWEN. Just 'cause she's tall and blonde and skinny doesn't give her the right to look down on all of us.

SUE. Yeah, who does she think she is anyway?

Scene   2

Setting. The family home. The kitchen. Late afternoon.

*(**BRIDGETTE** sits at the table, doing homework. **SHE** wears a cheerleading skirt and top. **SHE** is sniffling.)*

JACQUELYN. *(enters)* Hi, baby-girl. I didn't hear you come in.

*(**BRIDGETTE** doesn't respond. Keeping **HER** head down, **SHE** continues writing.)*

Did you get something to eat? Dinner's going to be a half an hour late.

(Silence.)

JACQUELYN. Bridgette….I'm speaking to you.
BRIDGETTE. *(mumbles)* I'm not hungry.
JACQUELYN. Okay. How was cheerleading practice today? Did you have fun?
BRIDGETTE. *(head still down)* It was okay.

*(**JACQUELYN** crosses over and puts her finger gently under **BRIDGETTE's** chin, raising **HER** face so **SHE** has to look at **HER** mother.)*

JACQUELYN. Look at me. What's wrong, honey? *(looking closer)* Have you been crying?
BRIDGETTE. *(Pulls her head away)* No!
JACQUELYN. Yes, you have.   What happened?
BRIDGETTE. Allergies. I've got a ton of homework.
JACQUELYN. You don't have allergies.
BRIDGETTE. I do now. Must be something in the walls of this new house.

JACQUELYN. Honey….I know how much you hated this move. But we had to…the promotion your Dad was offered required us to move here.

BRIDGETTE. He could have turned it down…

JACQUELYN. Now you know better. We've been through all this.

BRIDGETTE. My life is ruined. No one gets pulled out of their high school and forced to move. It's just not fair.

JACQUELYN. I know, baby, life is just *that* sometimes, unfair.

BRIDGETTE. I let my team down.

JACQUELYN. No, you didn't. We gave them plenty of notice. What's really wrong?

BRIDGETTE. The girls here are dumb and they're really mean.

JACQUELYN. Which girls?

BRIDGETTE. At school, on the new team…they call me names when I can hear them.

JACQUELYN. Oh, honey. Have you talked to them? Let them get to know the real you?

BRIDGETTE. No. They think I'm stuck up.

JACQUELYN. *(Laughs.)* If you….

BRIDGETTE. It's not funny!

JACQUELYN. If you're stuck up, then the moon is really made of blue cheese.

BRIDGETTE. They called me 'ice queen'.

JACQUELYN. Oh, sweetie…

BRIDGETTE. *(Forlorn.)* I don't care. I don't like them anyway.

JACQUELYN. They don't realize how shy you are…and coming into a new school doesn't help.

BRIDGETTE. I can't help that I'm shy. I get all tongue tied when I'm around new kids. Most of my friends at home I've known since kindergarten. **JACQUELYN.** Bridg…this is 'home' now. You've got to try.

BRIDGETTE. Fine. I'll try harder. Leave me alone.

JACQUELYN. No, I will not. As your Mom and your biggest fan it's my job to try and find a solution to the problem of your shyness and making some friends.

*(Pulling out a chair **JACQUELYN** sits across from **HER** daughter.)*

BRIDGETTE. *(Groans.)* Oh, brother…

 JACQUELYN. Is there at least one girl on the cheer squad that you like?

BRIDGETTE. Yeah, sort'a.

JACQUELYN. And what's her name?

BRIDGETTE. Annie. She's ridiculous.

JACQUELYN. That's a good thing, right?

BRIDGETTE. *(Sighing.)* Yes, Mom.

JACQUELYN. Well, why don't you take this one person at a time? Tomorrow at practice say 'hi' to Annie.

BRIDGETTE. And then what do I say? Assuming that she even answers me.

JACQUELYN. Tonight think of three things the two of you have in common and then write a script in your head so that you don't get tongue tied. If she says 'hi' back, be ready with a conversation.

BRIDGETTE. I don't know, Mom…

JACQUELYN. What have you got to lose? You say the girls are being standoffish now so what's the worst that can happen?

BRIDGETTE. Yeah, I guess I could talk to her about cheering, and we do have a chemistry class together.

JACQUELYN. See? That's two topics right there.

BRIDGETTE. What if she thinks I'm stuck up and doesn't say 'hi' back?

JACQUELYN. Just smile sincerely and say 'hi'. I know that she'll say 'hi' back and maybe something more. You be ready to jump right in with something about cheering or chemistry. Then she'll say something back and you can comment on that. It's called conversation, honey.

BRIDGETTE. You really think this might work?

JACQUELYN. Bridgette, you've got to start somewhere to try and overcome your shyness.

BRIDGETTE. How come those girls think I'm stuck up anyway? I've never been mean to them.

JACQUELYN. Maybe, because the appearance of being shy and being stuck up are very similar. A shy person doesn't look people in the eye, doesn't contribute to the conversation or make friends very easily. Someone who's stuck on themselves is aloof, thinks they're too good to talk to certain people and only has a few friends…because they're stuck up.

BRIDGETTE. When you put it that way I see how much alike they are. So what you're saying is because I'm shy, they think I'm stuck up?

JACQUELYN. Exactly. So be very brave and speak to Annie tomorrow and see what happens.

BRIDGETTE. Okay, I guess. *(Beat.)* I'm starved; can I have a yogurt and an apple?

JACQUELYN. If you promise to leave room for dinner.

(JACQUELYN rises and crosses to get her daughter a snack.)

BRIDGETTE. Thanks, Mom.

JACQUELYN. It's the least I can do….feed my child.

BRIDGETTE. No I mean about the other thing…the advice.

JACQUELYN. *(Shocked by her gratitude.)* Oh! You're welcome, sweetie. Don't forget to rehearse what you are going to say to Annie tomorrow.

BRIDGETTE. I won't.

JACQUELYN. Okay then.

Scene 3

Setting. School. The next day. Cheer practice.

(**ANNIE** *sits, tying her shoes. As* **SHE** *straightens up* **BRIDGETTE** *is approaching* **HER. ANNIE** *immediately looks up and smiles.*)

ANNIE. Hi!
BRIDGETTE. *(Stunned)* Umm…hi.
ANNIE. You're Bridgette, right?
BRIDGETTE. Yes, and you're Annie?
ANNIE. Yes. *(Beat)* Ready for practice?
BRIDGETTE. Always. I love cheerleading, don't you?
ANNIE. *(Laughing)* It's my life!
BRIDGETTE. *(Forgetting her 'script' she chokes.)* …Umm….
ANNIE. Aren't you in my chem' class?
BRIDGETTE. *(Feels like she's been thrown a life line)* YES!
ANNIE. The teacher's so lame.
BRIDGETTE. *(Sitting down.)* Yeah.
ANNIE. What did you get on last Friday's test?
BRIDGETTE. A 'C'. You?
ANNIE. B minus. *(Beat.)* Hey! Maybe we could study together, bring our grade up.
BRIDGETTE. Yeah, I'd like that.
ANNIE. Sick! Tomorrow after school?
BRIDGETTE. Yes, that's good.

ANNIE. Except it will have to be at your house, 'cause my parents work and I'm not allowed to have anyone in the house when they're not there.

BRIDGETTE. Parents. They're so lame.

ANNIE. I *know!*

BRIDGETTE. *(Tentative.)* My mom could pick us up after school and then take you home after….if you want.

ANNIE. That's sick.

BRIDGETTE. My Mom makes pretty good snacks.

ANNIE. I can always eat.

BRIDGETTE. …Ummm…well…

ANNIE. Can I tell you something?

BRIDGETTE. Sure.

ANNIE. The rest of the squad says you're stuck up.

BRIDGETTE. Yeah, I know.

ANNIE. I don't get it. You're not stuck on yourself at all.

BRIDGETTE. *(Desperate.)* I'm not, Annie. I *promise* I'm not.

ANNIE. You know what I think?

BRIDGETTE. *(Fearful.)* No. What?

ANNIE. I think you're just a little shy.

BRIDGETTE. Maybe a little.

(**THEY** *smile at each other.*)

VOICE. *(Off.)* Okay, squad! Listen up. One lap around to warm up.

ANNIE. *(Groaning and grinning.)* What a pain.

BRIDGETTE. I *know.*

Scene 4
(Optional Scene for larger cast)

Setting. School. The next day.

(GWEN, SUE, *and* **ANNIE** *are standing by their lockers in the hallway.)*

GWEN. *(Accusing.)* You were *talking* to her!
ANNIE. Who?
SUE. Bridgette.
GWEN. The Ice Queen.
ANNIE. Yeah?
SUE. She's stuck up.
GWEN. We don't like her.
ANNIE. No, she's not really. And Gwen, how can you say that? You don't even *know* her.
SUE. She always snubs us.
GWEN. *Nobody* on the squad likes her.
ANNIE. Well, I do. She's nice.
SUE. *(Gasps.)* How can you?
GWEN. She's weird.
ANNIE. No, she's *new*. She doesn't know anybody.
SUE. That's her fault.
GWEN. Yeah, we've given her plenty of chances.
ANNIE. *(Looking at both girls pointedly.)* Really? Have you?
SUE. *(Unsure.)* Of course. Haven't we Gwen?
GWEN. Well, it's your funeral if you befriend her, Annie.
ANNIE. *(Sardonically.)* Well, you might as well know the worst. I'm going to her house after school today to study.
SUE. You aren't!
GWEN. You can't.

ANNIE. I can. And I am.

SUE. But, Annie, everyone will call you 'stuck up' too.

GWEN. That's for sure.

ANNIE. Look! She's a nice girl and a really good cheerleader. She's good for our team. Coach said we might even try to go to regionals this year.

GWEN. I still don't like her.

ANNIE. You're starting to sound like a mean girl, Gwen.

GWEN. *(Glaring.)* I am not!

SUE. Well, I guess we could get to know her. Do you think if we sat with her at lunch she would snub us?

ANNIE. Absolutely not.

SUE. Are you sure she's not stuck up? I don't want to be embarrassed in front of everybody.

ANNIE. She is not stuck on herself. She's just shy. It's really hard for her to talk to new people.

SUE. What do you think, Gwen?

GWEN. I don't want anyone *(Looks at Annie.)* to think I'm a mean girl. But if she acts conceited and stuck up I'm outta there!

ANNIE. That's fair. But, I think you're going to be surprised at how nice Bridgette is.

SUE. Okay, I'm in too.

> *(A bell rings.)*

Oh, gosh, we're going to be late for class!

> **(ALL** *three girls rush off in different directions.)*

ANNIE. See you in the lunch room.

SUE. See you later.

GWEN. Whatever…

CURTAIN

THE POSTCARD

by

Trisha Sugarek

CAST OF CHARACTERS

Betsy - Mid-forties. The mother of Elizabeth.

Elizabeth - Early-twenties, she is the bride-to-be.

Joe - Elizabeth's fiancée. He is in his late twenties.

Scene   1

Setting. Family living room.

> [**BETSY** *sits with a cup of tea at her side.* **SHE** *is addressing envelopes. Humming the wedding march.* **ELIZABETH,** *her daughter, rushes through the front door,* **HER** *arms full of magazines, catalogs, and mail.* **SHE** *is like a pretty puppy, full of enthusiasm.]*

ELIZABETH. Mother!
BETSY. Here, darling.

> [**ELIZABETH** *whirls around and rushes to* **HER** *mother, waving the mail.]*

ELIZABETH. More wedding catalogs, Mom.   Wanna look at them now?
BETSY. Later, darling. You'd better get showered. Joe will be here in less than an hour.

> [**ELIZABETH** *grabs her mother's wrist to check the time.]*

ELIZABETH. Holy Smokes!   Where did the time go? We were having such fun with the menu for the reception, I had no idea it was so late.

> [**SHE** *begins to run from the room, all the mail still in* **HER** *hands.]*

See you in a minute, Mom.
BETSY. Lizzy-bug...
ELIZABETH. *[Stops and turns.]* Yes?
BETSY. The mail's going to get very wet.

*[Looking baffled **SHE** glances down at the mail in **HER** hands. **SHE** laughs. **SHE** rushes back and dumps all the mail into her mother's lap.]*

ELIZABETH. Oh! Right. Back soon.

*[**ELIZABETH** exits. **BETSY** begins to read the mail.]*

BETSY. *[To herself.]* Where in the world did I get a child like that?

*[Still humming the wedding march and going through a large amount of various envelopes, **BETSY** comes to a postcard with a colorful bunch of flowers on the back. **SHE** is visibly shaken and nervously turns the postcard over as if the flowers will solve the mystery.]*

BETSY. 'Dear Mom'…What? Why is Lizzy sending me a postcard?

*[**BETSY** reads aloud.]*

'Dear Mom…I hope you don't mind me calling you that. I don't know what to say…or where to begin, but I had to write you, now that I have found you.'

*[**BETSY** lays her head back on the chair. **SHE** lifts her head after a beat or two   and continues to read.]*

BETSY. 'Please, please don't rip this up until you've read it all. I so want to meet you, see you. I have ever since I was old enough to know what 'adopted' meant. Please call me at the number below….I'll be waiting. Love, Sally.'

*[**BETSY** stares at the postcard. The doorbell sounds. Rising and crossing to the door, **SHE** opens it to find **JOE**, Elizabeth's fiancée.]*

BETSY. Joe! *[They hug.]* How many times do I have to tell you? This is your home, so just walk right in.
JOE. I know, Betsy, I know. *[Laughing.]* My Mom's training keeps getting in the way.
BETSY. *[Crosses to her chair and sits.]* So after the wedding my new son is going to ring the doorbell like a…*[Laughs.]*… a vacuum salesman.
JOE. Who knows? If the market keeps going the way it has, I just might sell you a vacuum.
ELIZABETH. *[Off.]* Mom!
 BETSY. Darling….Joe's here.
ELIZABETH. *[Off.]* Hi, my love...
JOE. *[Calling to her.]* Hi, 'Lizzy-bug'!

ELIZABETH. Don't. Call. Me. That.   See what you've created Mom?
BETSY. *[Not sorry at all.]*   Sorry, darling.
ELIZABETH. *[Off.]* Be out in a jiffy. Mom, show Joe the menu.
JOE. Oh, no, please.   No more. I don't wanna see the menu.
BETSY. *[Laughing.]* Don't worry, I won't. There are some things that the groom just doesn't need to know.
JOE. Thank you! You're an angel of a mother-in-law.

> *[Indicating the next room.]*

 JOE. How's she doing?
BETSY. She's like a small, benign hurricane. And I've never seen her happier. You're good for her, Joe. So calm and unflappable. Thank you for that.
JOE. I promise I will remain so... *[Smiling fondly.]*..if I don't have to see the menu for the reception.
BETSY. It's a deal. When Lizzy asks you what you think, tell her you love it.

> *[A small silence;* **BETSY** *gazes out the window.* **JOE** *watches her.]*

JOE. How's the mother of the bride today?

> *[***BETSY*** *does not answer.]*

Earth calling Mom. I need to add one hundred names to the invite list. *[Teasing.]*

> *[***BETSY*** *jumps and focuses on JOE.]*

BETSY. Oh, sorry, dear. What were you saying?
JOE. Nothing. Just testing if you were in the room or not. You okay?
BETSY. Yes, certainly. Never better...

> *[***ELIZABETH*** *whirls into the room and as* **JOE** *stands,* **SHE** *throws* **HERSELF** *into his arms.* **THEY** *kiss.]*

ELIZABETH. Joey! I've missed you so much.
JOE. It's been six hours, Lizzy.
ELIZABETH. That long?
BETSY. Children, please sit down. I would like to discuss something with you...

> *[***ELIZABETH*** *is alert to her mother's moods.]*

ELIZABETH. What is it, Mom? What's wrong?

BETSY. I got a letter in the mail...well, not a letter, really. A postcard...

JOE. Why don't you two girls talk and I'll go in the kitchen and find myself a beer. You ladies want more tea?

BETSY. I'd like you to stay, please, Joe. Ever since Lizzy's father died, I find myself relying more and more on you.

ELIZABETH. Of course, you'll stay, Joey. You're part of our family... is it something to do with the wedding? I knew everything was going too smoothly...all my friends had the most terrible time planning their weddings...their mothers turned into monsters...the flowers didn't arrive on time...one bridesmaid gained a bunch of weight and couldn't get into her dress...why, Mary Jo's church was double booked!...Can you imagine?

BETSY. Elizabeth.

ELIZABETH. Sorry Mom. What is it?

BETSY. Now listen carefully, Lizzy, to what I am about to tell you. It changes nothing...NOTHING...you are still my best girl and I love you very much...

ELIZABETH. *[Tears fill her eyes.]* Oh my God! You've got cancer. I knew things were too good to be true. Daddy last year and now this...

BETSY. Darling, no, no...I'm fine. I'm not sick. It's just that I got this postcard and now I have to tell you something...

ELIZABETH. Oh, Mommy, you scared me. *[Beat.]* What's a dumb old postcard got to do with anything?

JOE. Lizzy, your Mom is trying to tell us. Maybe if you listen for a few, very short minutes, we'll understand.

ELIZABETH. Of course! How silly. My mouth is always running...I can't seem to help it.

BETSY. As you know, Lizzy, I started at the University when I was seventeen. In my sophomore year, I met a senior and fell madly in love.

ELIZABETH. Daddy?

BETSY. No dear. This was years before I met Dad. Anyway, six months later I found out that I was pregnant. I went to my boyfriend with the news. I thought he'd be happy about a baby. He would graduate before it was born and I would continue with my classes until I got further along. We'd be married and live happily ever after. *[Derisive laugh.]* My goodness, I couldn't have been more wrong. He disappeared from my life. If we happened to meet on campus, he didn't know me. It was so embarrassing. So, I transferred and finished the year out. When the baby was born, I gave it up for adoption.

ELIZABETH. Oh Mommy....

JOE. That was pretty brave of you, Mom.

BETSY. I don't know. Sometimes I think it was pretty cowardly of me. I was on full scholarship and still had to work two jobs just to get by. How could I support a baby too?

ELIZABETH. But, I don't see what this has got to do with my wedding....

JOE. I think I do. *[Beat.]* Let your Mom tell us the rest, Lizzy.

BETSY. In the mail...today...I got this postcard...from *her*.

*[**BETSY** holds it up for **THEM** to see.]*

ELIZABETH. From who? Oh! *Her*? *[Beat.]* You mean you had another daughter?
BETSY. Yes, dear. A daughter, your sister, Sally.
ELIZABETH. *[Gasps and grabs Joe's hand.]*
NO! Absolutely not! You're *my* mother...*[Begins to cry.]*....you're not hers!

*[**BETSY** rises and crosses to **ELIZABETH**. **SHE** sits on the other side of her.]*

BETSY. Of course I'm your mother, Lizzy-bug. I love you best, always.   You're my own sweet girl...
ELIZABETH. What does she want?
BETSY. She wants us to meet.   You may read the note if you wish.
ELIZABETH. No! I don't want you to meet her. *[Inconsolable.]*   She's nothing to us....she's not your daughter, I AM! How could you?
JOE. Easy, honey.
BETSY. How could I what, Lizzy?
ELIZABETH. Everything! *[Hysterical.]* Get pregnant! Give your baby away! Not tell me!
[Beat.]   Why didn't you tell me? We tell each other *everything*. You said so...
BETSY. I didn't tell you because it was so long ago. I never imagined that it would touch our lives. I knew that she had gone to good people who would take care of her and love her...
ELIZABETH. Stop calling her, 'her'. She's got a name. Sally.
BETSY. Yes...Sally.
 ELIZABETH. She's real. *[Beat.]* Oh, my God, she's real.
JOE. What're you going to do, Mom?
BETSY. I don't know. What do you want me to do, baby?
ELIZABETH. *[She rises, still crying, and crosses to the door.]* It's not up to me, it's not!   You have to decide. She seems to think that she's your daughter ...but whatever you do... don't tell me...I don't want to know...she's not part of my life.

*[**ELIZABETH** exits.]*

BETSY. *[Sighing.]* Go to her, Joe. She needs you.

*[As **BETSY** rises, **JOE** rises and takes **BETSY** into a loose embrace.]*

JOE. It's going to be okay, Mom. Just let Elizabeth get used to the idea...the stress of the wedding...It's been a huge shock for everyone...especially you. *[Beat.]* I'd better go and find her.
BETSY. Yes, darling...*[As Joe exits.]* and Joe?
JOE. Yes.

BETSY. Thank you, my boy.
JOE. Don't thank me. It's my job as your favorite son-in-law. Don't worry, okay Mom?

*[**JOE** exits. **BETSY** sits back down in her chair. Almost immediately, **JOE** and **ELIZABETH** come back into the room. **ELIZABETH**'s head is down. **THEY** walk to the   front door.]*

JOE. Mom, we're going for a ride, maybe catch a movie. We won't be late. See you later.
BETSY. All right, my darlings. Be careful. Have fun.

*[**BETSY** sits quietly in the chair. **SHE** picks up the post card and reads it again. Looks at the phone on a side table by the sofa. **SHE** rises and crosses to the phone. Referring to the postcard dials.]*

BETSY. Hello...yes, I'd like to speak to Sally, please. This is Betsy Graves calling...Oh! It's you... Sally...this is your...

CURTAIN

The Bullies

by

Trisha Sugarek

Cast of Characters

Aamir............A teen born in the USA, his family is
from India.   In his first year of high school,
he is on the varsity debate team and a state champion
in Chess.

Taggart "Tag"....A junior in high school, a football star,
and a bully.

Steve............One of Tag's friends and followers.

Jimmy..........Another friend of Tag's, a football line-backer. He reluctantly follows the gang but his instincts tell him that bullying is not right.

Voice. (Dr. Chandak)......Aamir's father is a physicist and came to the US before Aamir was born. He has a very slight accent in his speech patterns.

Author's Notes: 'Every day thousands of teens wake up afraid to go to school. Bullying is a problem that affects millions of students, and it has everyone worried, not just the kids on its receiving end. Yet because parents, teachers, and other adults don't always see it, they may not understand how extreme bullying can get.

Bullying is when a person is picked on over and over again by an individual or group with more power, either in terms of physical strength or social standing. Two of the main reasons people are bullied are because of appearance and social status. Bullies pick on the people they think don't fit in, maybe because of how they look, how they act (for example, kids who are shy and withdrawn), their race or religion, or because the bullies think their target may be gay or lesbian.

Verbal bullying can also involve sending cruel instant or email messages or even posting insults about a person on a website — practices that are known as cyber bullying.' Courtesy of: http://kidshealth.org/teen/your_mind/problems/bullies.html

Production Notes

  Aamir is pronounced 'Ah-mear'.
The ethnic slurs, as they relate to countries, are incorrect on purpose. These young boys are throwing out slurs randomly and don't know where Aamir is from.

The 'N' word and 'faggot' can be substituted; but consider the fact that this is part of teen racism and bullying.

The use of a double set, such as it is, is still kept simple and may be changed at the director's discretion.
Tenses and incorrect English by the boys is intentional. The name calling is important to the dramatic effect and impact to accurately illustrate how vicious bullying can be. They can be substituted at the director's discretion.

Scene   1

Setting. School. Friday afternoon.

> [**AAMIR** *sits in front of a computer screen working on* **HIS** *homework. A chime sounds that a message is coming in.* **AAMIR** *clicks on the window.*]

AAMIR. *[Reads aloud.]* 'We know you're a terrorist so go back to where you come from. We don't want your filth in our town.' Wow! That was bizarre-o! Wonder where that came from.

> [*A chime sounds again indicating another message.* **AAMIR** *stares at the computer screen. HE doesn't open the window.*]

****

> [*Across the stage, opposite* Aamir, *three boys are grouped around a computer.* **TAGGERT** *is at the keyboard.* **STEVE** *and* **JIMMY** *are laughing and* **STEVE** *is egging "TAG" on.*]

STEVE. Write another one, Tag.
TAGGART. *[Laughing.]* The little faggot opened that one. Here's a new one.

> [*As* **HE** *types,* **HE** *reads the message out loud to* **HIS** *buddies.*]

'We don't want you Muslim slant-eyes in our country. Go home! If you don't, you'll be sorry.' *[Clicks to send.]*

> [**STEVE** *and* **TAGGART** *laugh more.*]

JIMMY. *[Uncomfortable.]* Hey, guys! This is boring. Let's go throw a football around.

TAGGART. Are you nuts? This is the best fun I've had all week. *[Laughs.]* It is our duty, as US citizens to root out evil wherever we find it! *[Typing again.]* Let's see how he likes this one. *[Reading aloud.]* 'You better not be in school on Monday. We'll be waiting for you. We got a little surprise for you that you won't like.'

STEVE. *[Laughs.]* Oh yeah, that'll scare the crap outta the little four-eyes.

[**AAMIR** *can't resist opening the two new messages.* **HE** *reads them aloud.* **HE** *makes a disgusted noise and closes* **HIS** *laptop.*]

AAMIR. *[Muttering..]* What a bunch of sickos. You'd think they had better things to do.

DR. CHANDAK. *[Off.]* Aamir, come on, we will be late for your chess competition. Traffic will be bad. Hurry, now.

AAMIR. Coming, Dad.

[**AAMIR** *rushes from the room. Exits.*]

Scene   2

Setting. Aamir's home. Sunday afternoon.

[**AAMIR** *sits at* **HIS** *desk, text books around* **HIS** *computer.   A chime alerts that a message is coming in.*]

AAMIR. *[Sighing.]* What now?

[**HE** *clicks on the window.* **HE** *reads the message and then begins typing furiously. Speaking aloud as* **HE** *types.*]

'Who are you?'

[*Across the room* **TAGGART** *sits at* **HIS** *computer and types back, reading aloud as* **HE** *types.*]

TAGGART. 'Your worst nightmare. Ready for school tomorrow, douche-bag?

[*Across the room,* **AAMIR** *reads the screen and begins to type.*]

AAMIR. Who are you!?
TAGGART. *[Typing.]* You'll find out if you've got the cachones to come to school tomorrow.
AAMIR. *[Typing.]* I'm not afraid of you. You're a coward, you know that? Hiding behind a computer.
TAGGART. *[Typing.]* We'll see who's the coward when you go running away screaming like a little girl. See ya tomorrow, slant-eyes.

[*Simultaneously, both* **BOYS** *close* **THEIR** *laptops.*]

DR. CHANDAK. *[Off.]* Aamir! Come down now, dinner is prepared.

AAMIR. *[Rises, walks to the door of his room and yells back.]* I'm not hungry, Dad. I'll eat later.

DR. CHANDAK. *[Off.]* You will come now, son. Your mother worked ever so hard to prepare a family feast. You will not disappoint her.

AAMIR. *[Sighing.]* Be right down, Dad.

[Exits.]

Scene   3

Setting. School.   The next day.

> [**AAMIR** *is walking to* **HIS** *next class.* **TAGGART, STEVE** *and* **JIMMY** *are walking towards* **AAMIR**. *As the* **BOYS** *pass* **TAGGART** *bumps into* **AAMIR** *hard.]*

AAMIR. *[Polite.]* Oh, sorry. Guess I wasn't watching where I was going.

> [**HE** *tries to walk on. The three other* **BOYS** *surround* **AAMIR**.*]*

TAGGART.   You talkin' to me, nigger?

> [**STEVE** *giggles nervously at the 'n' word *See notes.* **JIMMY** *gasps at how far* **TAGGART** *is taking this.]*

TAGGART. *[Shoving him again.]* Answer me, boy!
AAMIR. You're him….the one that's been sending me messages.
TAGGART.   *[Laughing, he turns to his buddies.]* The guy's a genius, figured it out all by himself that it was us.
STEVE.   *[Punches Aamir on the arm.]* A real genius. Pretty smart for a black boy.
AAMIR. I am not African-American, I am Indian.

> [**TAGGART** *begins to hoot and holler and starts what* **HE** *believes to be a Native-American dance.* **STEVE** *follows* **HIS** *lead.* **JIMMY** *stands off to the side watching.]*

TAGGART. Woo, woo, woo, woo.

*[**AAMIR** starts to walk off.]*

TAGGART. Hey! Where ya goin'? *[Blocking Aamir's path.]* Did I say you could leave?
AAMIR. I will be late for class.
TAGGART. Oh, boo-hoo, he's going to be late for class.
JIMMY. So are we, Tag. We can't be late again or we'll be benched Friday night.
TAGGART. *[Gets in Jimmy's face.]* Did I ask you for your opinion?
JIMMY. No.
STEVE. But, he's right, Tag. Coach warned us.
TAGGART. Yeah, like Coach is gonna bench *me*, the starting quarterback? Riiiight!

*[**TAGGART** turns to **AAMIR** and punch-shoves **HIM** in the chest.]*

TAGGART. Ya got off easy this time, Genius. Scamper off to class like a good little gook.

*[The three **BOYS** saunter off, laughing. **AAMIR** picks **HIS** books off the ground and walks away in the opposite direction.]*

****

*[Later that day **AAMIR** sits at his computer. **HIS** cell phone rings.]*

AAMIR. Hello? Oh, Hi, Derek. What're you doing?.... No I haven't been on FaceBook for a couple of days, why?.... Really?.....About me?.....Hold on….*[Aamir types and clicks as he talks.]* I'm bringing it up now. Whose wall?.....OK.

*[**AAMIR** reads aloud while Derek is still on the phone.]*

AAMIR. A terrorist just waiting to strike? A secret Muslim cell right here in our midst?.....*[Derek is talking.]*... No, of course it's not true. Gosh, Derek, you've known me since fourth grade. Besides, I'm not even Saudi Arabian or Afgantianian, I'm Indian …..I'm not even Muslim. …I don't know what I'm going to do. Probably just ignore it……Yeah, catch ya later, bye.

*[**AAMIR** sits, staring at **HIS** computer screen.]*

AAMIR. Wow. This is so weird.

Scene   4

Setting. The school. Later that week.

> [**AAMIR** *is walking to the room where his   chess club plays.* **HE** *is carrying the box that holds his chess pieces.* **TAGGART, STEVE** *and* **JIMMY** *are waiting around a corner. As* **AAMIR** *walks by* **THEY** *surround* **AAMIR**. **TAGGART** *knocks the box out of* **AAMIR**'S *hands and scoops it up.]*

AAMIR. Hey. That's mine. Give it back.
TAGGART. Not anymore.
STEVE. Yeah, it's ours now.

> [**TAGGART** *opens the box, all the time avoiding* **AAMIR**'s *attempts to get it back.* **TAGGART** *pulls out a very beautiful, wood carved chess piece from India.]*

AAMIR. Don't touch those.
STEVE. Who's gonna stop us?
TAGGART. Hey, guys, look at the little statue. What does the Bible say about graven images? You worship graven images back in the jungles where you come from, four-eyes?
AAMIR. Those are chess pieces, Taggart. *Not* graven images. Now give them back!
TAGGART. Why should I?
STEVE. Yeah, why should he?
JIMMY. Come on, Tag, give 'em back. We're gonna be late for practice.
TAGGART. Shut up, Jimmy. *[To Aamir.]* So what's the deal? Is this where you hide the explosives? Let's crack one open and see.
STEVE. Yeah.
AAMIR. NO! My father gave me that chess set.

*[AAMIR makes a grab for the box and inadvertently strikes **TAGGART** in the chest. Everyone is absolutely still for a couple of beats.]*

TAGGART. Oh no, you didn't…just hit me.
 AAMIR. Sorry. It was an accident. Please return my chess box.

*[**TAGGART** tosses the box to **STEVE** and rushes **AAMIR**.]*

TAGGART. Did you just hit me, ya little faggot?

*[**HE** begins to strike **AAMIR** in the face and body. **AAMIR** tries to cover **HIS** face and finally falls to the ground and curls up. **TAGGART** leans over him.]*

TAGGART. Huh? You want to fight me?? You got it, ya little douche-bag! *[Hit.]* Gook! *[Hit.]* Slant-eyes! *[Hit.]* You don't belong here. America is for Americans!

*[**TAGGART** doesn't appear to be able to stop hitting. **JIMMY** pulls **HIM** off.]*

JIMMY. Tag! That's enough. Cut it out! We're gonna get into trouble. Come on, stop!

*[**JIMMY** pulls **TAGGART** away. **AAMIR** stays on the ground. **TAGGART** swaggers over to **STEVE**. **HE** takes the box from **STEVE** and throws it down on top of **AAMIR**. Chess pieces scatter everywhere.]*

TAGGART. Come on, guys, let's get outta here. I gotta wash my hands after touching this weirdo.

*[**TAGGART** and **STEVE** saunter off, laughing together as **THEY** exit. **JIMMY** stays behind. Slowly, **JIMMY** begins to pick up the chess pieces and puts them back into the box. **AAMIR** sits up when **HE** sees that only **JIMMY** remains, **HE** stands.]*

JIMMY. *[Handing over the box.]* Here, I'm not sure I found them all.
AAMIR. *[Aamir checks the pieces in the box.]* There's two missing.

*[The **BOYS** look around and each find one of the missing pieces. **JIMMY** hands the piece to **AAMIR**.]*

AAMIR. Thanks.
JIMMY. 'Welcome. *[Beat.]* Your cheek is bleeding.

*[**AAMIR** takes out a white handkerchief and wipes **HIS** face.]*

Does it hurt?

AAMIR. Not too much. But my ribs hurt like the devil.

[**JIMMY** *laughs nervously. And after a moment,* **AAMIR** *joins in.*]

AAMIR. Owww.

JIMMY. Look. I'm sorry, okay? This got way out of hand.

AAMIR. Yeah.

JIMMY. We were just horsing around on the computer, teasing guys, not just you. Then, well, Tag….I don't know….he kinda got all focused on you for some reason. *[Beat.]* I'm sorry you got beat up. I had no idea it was going to go this far.

AAMIR. I'm not a terrorist.

JIMMY. I know. Tag just made that up.

AAMIR. Why me? Abdallah and Nadim both go to our school and they're from Saudi.

JIMMY. Yeah, except they're…..

AAMIR. Football players.

JIMMY. And bigger than Tag. I don't think he would mess with *them*. *[Beat.]* Are you going to report this to the office?

AAMIR. And be a snitch besides being a terrorist?

[**THEY** *both laugh.*]

I don't think so. I'm so clumsy, I keep running into locker doors.

JIMMY. I just want you to know that I was pretty uncomfortable with some of the names Tag called you. That's not what I think at all.

AAMIR. Yeah, I know. Where'd he learn all that hate?

JIMMY. His Dad, I think. The first time his Dad saw Abdallah and Nadim at practice he went ballistic. Threatened to pull Tag off the football team. He called them a lot of the names Tag called you. It was crazy, man. *[Beat. Looks at his watch.]* Jeesch, look at the time, I'm am so late. Coach is gonna kill me!

AAMIR. Yeah, me too. I didn't mean…not the coach….the chess club, I mean. They are so punctual.

[**THEY** *laugh again and* **JIMMY** *puts his hand out to shake.* **AAMIR** *looks at it and then shakes* **JIMMY** *'s hand.* **THEY** *grin at each other over the hand shake.*]

AAMIR. See ya around.

JIMMY. Yeah, see ya.

[**THEY** *both exit in different directions.*]

Scene   5

Setting.   A classroom.

*[**JIMMY** is working on some poster board at a table. **AAMIR** enters. Walking up **HE** looks over **JIMMY**'s shoulder.]*

AAMIR. Wow! Look at that!
JIMMY. What do you think?
AAMIR. Do your jock friends know that you're such a good artist?
JIMMY. Gosh, no. Do you think I want to get beat up?

*[**JIMMY** holds up the poster. It is an almost completed poster that reads: "STUDENTS AGAINST VIOLENCE" "Stop the Bullying NOW!"]*

AAMIR. I just talked to two more kids that want to join our anti-bullying program.
JIMMY. How many does that make now?
AAMIR. Seventy-four at last count. And Principal Anderson is going to let us speak at the next student assembly.
JIMMY. I'll leave the speaking to you.
AAMIR. And I'll leave the drawing to you.
JIMMY. Deal. *[Laughing.]* You can't draw a straight line.
AAMIR. It sure didn't hurt our cause when Tiffany joined. She's only about the most popular girl in the entire school district. Who would have thought that she was bullied in grade school?
JIMMY. Go figure. She's so smart and pretty. What kind'a creep would bully her? *[Beat.]* Are Tag and Steve leaving you alone, Aamir?
AAMIR. Oh yeah. *[Laughing.]* I guess my black eye and scabby face scared them off.
JIMMY. And they respect you, in spite of themselves, for not telling. *[Beat.]* Word is they have their sights on some other guy. His name is Jacob. Do you know him?
AAMIR. Nope.

JIMMY. He's new here. I've talked to him and am encouraging him to join our program. Hopefully, we will get so many members that being a bully will no longer be the cool thing to do.

AAMIR. These guys need some counseling. *[He flips open his notebook.]*

JIMMY. Wha'cha writing?

AAMIR. A reminder to address the bullies in my speech. Did you know that Mrs. Hendrickson took some extra classes about counseling bullies? I met with her last week and she gave me some terrific ideas about our program. She's agreed to be our teacher mentor.

JIMMY. *[Embarrassed.]* Yeah, I know. I'm seeing her once a week.

AAMIR. You are? What for?

JIMMY. Remember, Aamir? Not so long ago *I* was the bully.

CURTAIN

The Bard of the Yukon

by

Trisha Sugarek

CAST OF CHARACTERS

La Verne - The youngest sister of thirteen kids. She is barely sixteen and she yearns for adventure.

Robert Service - the ghost of Robert Service. La Verne and he are great friends.

Ivah - Her older sister. She is almost nineteen and engaged to be married.

Violet - Just eighteen, she is the sultry beauty of the family.

Author's note: Robert Service's poems are found in "The Best of Robert Service" Publisher: Dodd, Mead & Company, New York.

Inspired by a true story, LaVerne did go to Alaska and did write her songs.

Scene   1

Setting. 1920. Late one night in the Guyer household.

[LA VERNE shares a room with her two older sisters, IVAH and VIOLET, are asleep in the larger of two beds. LA VERNE lies on her bed, on the top of the blankets, while MR. SERVICE sits in a rocker. LA VERNE is dressed in a floor length night-gown. A duffle bag lies, almost out of sight, at the end of the bed. A single oil lantern burns to light the room. LA VERNE, listens raptly to MR. SERVICE.]

MR. SERVICE.*[Reciting his own poetry.]*'A bunch of the boys were whooping it up in the Malamute saloon; the kid that handles the music-box was hitting a jag-time tune;
Back of the bar, in a solo game, sat Dangerous Dan McGrew, And watching his luck was his light-o'-love, the lady that's known as Lou.
When out of the night, which was fifty below, and into the din and the glare,
There stumbled a miner fresh from the creeks, dog-dirty, and loaded for bear.
He looked like a man with a foot in the grave and scarcely the strength of a louse,
Yet he tilted a poke of dust on the bar, and he called for drinks for the house.
There was none could place the stranger's face, though we search ourselves for a clue;
But we drank his health, and the last to drink was Dangerous Dan McGrew.'...
..now, little one, go to sleep.
LA VERNE. No, no, Robert. I'm not the least bit sleepy. Skip to my favorite part of your poem...please?
MR. SERVICE. What part is that?

LA VERNE. 'Were you ever out in the Great Alone, when the moon was awful clear'.....finish it, please?

MR. SERVICE. '...And the icy mountains hemmed you in with a silence you most could hear; With only the howl of a timber wolf, and you camped there in the cold,
A half-dead thing in the stark, dead world, clean mad for the muck called gold; While high overhead, green, yellow, and red, the North Lights swept in bars?-
Then you've a hunch what the music meant...hunger and night and the stars.

   *[**THEY** both fall silent.]*

VI. *[Raising up on one elbow and whispers.]* La Verne! Wake up! You're talking in your sleep again! Shut up and go to sleep.

   *[**VI** flounces onto her side and buries **HERSELF** in the covers.]*

LA VERNE. *[Whispers.]* What most inspired you, Robert, about Alaska? The harshness of the landscape? The doing without...the hardships?

MR. SERVICE. No, no. I think it was the complete lack of concern by Mother Nature. You could live or die; she had far more important things to attend to. The stillness and purity of being totally alone out on the tundra.

LA VERNE. You want to hear my most favorite?

MR. SERVICE. Will you go to sleep after?

   *[**LA VERNE** ignores the question and begins reciting.]*

LA VERNE. 'Men of the High North, the wild sky is blazing, Islands of opal float on silver seas;
Swift splendors kindle, barbaric amazing; Pale ports of amber, golden argosies.
Ringed all around us the proud peaks are glowing; Fierce chiefs in council, their wigwams the sky;
Far, far below us the big Yukon flowing,
Like threaded quicksilver, gleams to the eye.'

   *[**LA VERNE** rises and goes to the window and gazes out.]*

....and then my next favorite part.....

'Can you remember your huskies all going, barking with joy and their brushes in air; 'You in your parka, glad-eyed and glowing, Monarch, your subjects the wolf and the bear. Monarch, your kingdom unravished and gleaming;
Mountains your throne, and a river your car; Crash of a bull moose to rouse you from dreaming;
Forest your couch, and your candle a star.

You who this faint day the High North is luring unto her vastness, taintlessly sweet; You who are steel-braced, straight-lipped, enduring, Dreadless in danger and dire in defeat; Honor the High North ever and ever, Whether she crown you, or whether she slay; Suffer her fury, cherish and love her-- He who would rule he must learn to obey.'

> *[LA VERNE turns back to Mr. Service.]*

LA VERNE. That's what I want, Robert, to rule and obey.
MR. SERVICE. Someday, little one, some day.

> *[HE rises and disappears. LA VERNE lies down but is soon tossing and turning. A few beats later SHE jumps out of bed and strips off HER night gown. Under it SHE is fully clothed. SHE puts on a heavy coat and a hat. SHE picks up her boots and duffle bag. SHE crosses to the large bed and pokes HER sister's shoulder.]*

LA VERNE. Ivah...Ivah! Wake up.
IVAH. Umm...go away...it can't be morning yet. *[she cracks one eye open.]* It's still dark out. Are you crazy, La Verne? Go back to bed this instant!
LA VERNE. Please, Ivy, wake up for just a minute.   This is really important. Really, really important.
IVAH. What is it?

> *[Hearing something in her sister's voice, IVAH sits up.]*

This better be important or you are dead.   What?
VI. *[Mumbling.]*   Shut up, Ivah! Or you are dead!
IVAH. Oh yeah? And whose gonna make me? Not you...
LA VERNE. Shh...will you two be quiet? You're going to have the whole house in here.
VI. *[Burying her head in her pillow.]*   Gladly. Get back to bed you two.

> *[IVAH sits up in the bed, she plumps the pillows behind her.]*

 IVAH. Okay, squirt, what's so earth shattering that it can't wait 'till the morning?
LA VERNE. I'm leaving....I couldn't go without telling someone...I didn't want Mama to worry...
IVAH. Leaving? What'd ya mean?

> *[IVAH finally takes in the Scene   and sees LA VERNE is dressed and sees the duffle bag, all packed.]*

What the h-e-double toothpicks is going on? You've got a coat on...what's in the duffle?
What do you mean, you're leaving?
LA VERNE. I'm leaving...for the Yukon...tonight.
IVAH. Yukon? You mean in Alaska!?   Are you nuts? Go back to bed. That's it! You're sleep
walking...or I am.

[LA VERNE pinches IVAH hard.]

Ow..ow...what did you do that for?
LA VERNE. You are not sleep walking and neither am I. I just wanted to say goodbye.
IVAH. Vi! Wake up this instant! La Verne thinks she's running away.

[Pushes VI's shoulder hard.]

Wake up!
 VI. *[Rolls over and leans up on an elbow.]* What the devil is going on? La Verne, why do you have
your coat on?
IVAH. She's leaving, you slug. Wake up, I need your help.
VI. La Verne, take your coat off this instant and go back to bed. You're not going anywhere.
You're the baby, remember?
 IVAH. Shut up, Vi, and listen.
VI .*[Too loudly.]*   Who are you telling to shut up?
LA VERNE. Please...you're going to wake up Mama. Maybe I better just go...
IVAH. No, no!

[IVAH pokes VI with her elbow.]

VI. Ow...stop poking me!
IVAH. Vi, La Verne has a problem, that's obvious. Let's be good sisters and hear her out. What's
going on squirt?
VI. Yeah, spill it so we can go to sleep. It can't be that bad, Vernie.
LA VERNE. I've been thinking about this for a long time. I've read gobs on Alaska and that's the
place for me.
LA VERNE. You can chase your dreams there, be whoever you want to be...no one's going to tell
you what to do and what not to do...
 VI. Let's get practical for a moment. How are you going to get to Alaska? Do you have any idea
how far away it is?
LA VERNE. Oh, yes, I've done the research. I'm going to hitch a ride up to Seattle. Then I am
going to sign on a freighter, working my way to Alaska. *[Sighing.]* That's how Robert Service got
there.

IVAH. Just one little problem, Vernie. Robert Service was a guy. Who's going to hire a girl to work on a ship?

LA VERNE. I'm not going as a girl, dummy. I'm going to cut my hair and wear Eddie's old clothes. That way I can sign on as a kitchen helper or steward...I think that's what they call them. By the time they find out I'm a girl, either they won't care or it will be too late to turn back.

VI. Of all the hair brained ideas, Vernie, this takes the prize. *[She flops down in disgust.]* Go to bed.

IVAH. Hold on there, Vi. Let's hear Vernie out. *[To Laverne.]* What's wrong, squirt? Why are you leaving us?

VI. Not that I wouldn't love to be rid of a pesky little sister.

LA VERNE. Everybody's leaving... Lillas got married and is having a baby. *[To Ivah.]* You just got engaged and when you get married you'll be gone. And Vi's on her way to San Francisco to play basketball. Everybody's having an adventure except me. I don't want to be left here all alone.

IVAH. You'll still have Pa and Mama...and the boys when they come home for visits.

LA VERNE. That's different. I won't have any sisters here. *[Beat.]* I'll be the only girl. Besides, I feel like...well...

IVAH. What? You feel like what?

LA VERNE. Different from you. I want different things.

VI. Oh, everyone feels like that at your age. I thought I was adopted, for a whole year when I was fourteen. It was the worst year of my life.

IVAH. You're just growing up, Vernie.

LA VERNE. No it's more than that. Different...

IVAH. How?

LA VERNE. *[Looks at Vi.]* I'm afraid you'll laugh at me.

IVAH. No, I promise we won't. Don't we promise, Vi?

LA VERNE. Vi will laugh. She always laughs at me.

IVAH. Vi promises not to laugh. *[Pokes VI again.]* Promise her, Vi!

VI. Okay. I promise not to laugh, Vernie. Now what is it?

LA VERNE. I want to go to Alaska and write songs.

[VI sputters, trying to keep her promise.]

LA VERNE. See? She's laughing. I knew she would!

VI. No, no...I'm not...it was just a cough.

IVAH. Just ignore Vi. You know how she is. Everything is funny except when it comes to her life.

VI. That's not true...

LA VERNE. Shhh...!!

IVAH. Vernie, I know you love your music and writing and all. I love the songs that you've played for me. But, can't you write them here? Mama loves your music.

LA VERNE. No. To be a great writer, you have to suffer. When Mr. Service went to Alaska, he got very sick and had to come home. It took him years to get better. *[Loving the gore of it all.]* He got dysentery, lice, and he almost died from pneumonia.

VI. Holy Christopher! You're going to Alaska to suffer? Stay at home and I promise to make your life miserable every day. Now! Can we go back to sleep, please? *[Sighs.]* Good grief.

LA VERNE. You're mean, you know that Vi? I knew you wouldn't understand. I'm sorry I ever woke you up and told you.

VI. So am I, believe me, so am I.

LA VERNE. *[Wailing.]* I...vah!

IVAH. Never mind her. We all know how selfish Vi can be. Just ignore her. *[Beat.]* Vernie, have you thought about Mama? She is going to be so worried and hurt.

LA VERNE. That's why I woke you up, Ivy. I thought maybe you could talk to her after I'm gone. Make her understand. Tell her not to worry.

IVAH. Telling her not to worry is like telling the sun not to set. She'll never understand. You're her baby, Vernie.

LA VERNE. See? That's just it...I'm the 'baby'. I've been the 'baby' my whole life. I don't get to do anything. *[Beat.]* I'm going all the way to Nome.

LA VERNE. Just like Robert, I want to see the Aurora Boreattics, the...

IVAH. Borealis...

LA VERNE. Huh?

IVAH. It's Aurora Borealis.

LA VERNE. Yeah, that. The wolves and the glaciers and polar bears, and the streams filled with gold. Did you know that Robert Service rode with the mail carriers on their dog sleds? He traveled over a hundred miles with them delivering the mail and writing his poetry...

VI. He's a man! Men do stupid and dangerous stuff like that.

LA VERNE. I don't care. I'm going to ride with the mail and write my songs.

VI. Good grief. *[She flops over and pulls the covers up over her head.]* There's no talking to her.

IVAH. Do something for me, Vernie?

LA VERNE. I'm leaving...you can't talk me out of...

IVAH. No...I'm not going to try and talk you out of anything. I just want you to wait one day...okay? Let me think about all of this. I didn't know that what our sisters and I are doing was upsetting you so much. We've all been so wrapped up in our own lives and plans we haven't given much thought to how you must be feeling.

LA VERNE. Oh, Ivy, please don't blame yourself. This is something I have been dreaming about ever since I was a little kid...I want an adventure...a big one!

VI. *[From under the covers.]* Good grief.

LA VERNE. *[Outraged.]* Okay for you, Vi. Everything is just perfect for you! You get to go to a big city, play your stupid ball game, show off in front of a bunch of men. Probably fall in love like everyone else around here and get married....

[*VIOLET sits up, shocked by* **LA VERNE***'s words.*]

VI. Whoa! I didn't mean anything by what I said. I just meant....
IVAH. Oh, shut up, will you, Vi?
VI. Oh, like you know everything. Just because you're marrying a big shot lawyer doesn't make you the Queen of the World...
LA VERNE. Well, she sure knows more than you do Vi.
VI. Well, thanks very much.   See if I bring you anything when I come back from Frisco...
IVAH. Anyway, Vernie. Will you promise? Wait one more day, okay? Just one day.

[**LA VERNE** *has put her hands behind her back and upon this request from* **IVAH, SHE** *crosses her fingers before* **SHE** *promises.*]

LA VERNE. Well...Okay, Ivy, I promise.
IVAH. Good girl! Now let's all get back to bed. I'll see you in the morning, squirt.
VI. [*Already half asleep. On a big yawn.*]   'Night.
LA VERNE. I have to go to the 'necessary'.   I'll be right back.
IVAH. [*Snuggles under the quilt.*]   Do you want me to go with you?
LA VERNE. No thank you. I'll be fine.
IVAH. Hurry back. Don't let the bears get you.

[**LA VERNE** *exits standing at the bedroom door.*]

IVAH. Vi...Vi! You awake?
VI. Um-huh.
IVAH. Can you believe it? Vernie thinking she can get to Alaska? Of all the crazy ideas.
VI. Um-huh.
IVAH. You are going to have to help me talk her out of it. [*Silence.*]Vi? Violet Marie!   Answer me.
VI. Um-huh?
IVAH. Are you going to help or not?
VI. Yess!   Now leave me alone and go to sleep.

[A few beats. The girls have fallen asleep. **MR. SERVICE** *enters and sits in the rocking chair. The bedroom door opens and* **LA VERNE** *enters. Carrying her shoes,* **SHE** *crosses to her bed and sits down, fully clothed.]*

MR. SERVICE. So, what are you going to do? I strongly urge you to dream your dreams for a few more years before you actually go...

LA VERNE. No. It's time. I feel it. I can't wait. It's like what you said in Dauntless Quest...

'Why join the reckless, roving crew of trail and tent?
Why grimly take the roads of rue, to doom hell-bent?'

'Columbus, Cook and Cabot knew, and yet they went.'
... Can you understand?

MR. SERVICE. More than you know. You remind me of myself at your age.

[Beat.]

LA VERNE. *[Turns to her sisters in the bed.]* Ivah? Vi? I've been thinking about what you said. I think you're right. I couldn't possibly get to Alaska by myself. Ivy? Are you awake? Vi? *[Beat.]* Okay then.

*[**LA VERNE** rises and picks up* **HER** *shoes and duffle.* **SHE** *quietly crosses to the door then turns back.]*

LA VERNE. Goodbye. I love you both. Kiss Mama for me.

*[**SHE** exits.* **MR. SERVICE** *rises and starts to exit.]*

MR. SERVICE. *[To the sleeping forms in the bed.]* She won't be alone. *[Sighs.]* I shall be with her. *[Beat.]* Vernie, wait for me.

CURTAIN

YOU'RE NOT the   **BOSS** of ME

by

Trisha Sugarek

CAST OF CHARACTERS

Molly - 14 years old. The daughter.

Mother - 37 years old. A single Mom.

Bethany -15 years old. The most popular girl in school.

Optional: Various girls and boys - 15-17

Production note: (Expanded Scene) The 'slumber' party can be cast with more actors or use music, noise, and lights off stage to represent the party.

Scene   1

Setting. The living room.

[MOLLY's *mother sits on the sofa.* MOLLY *is sitting on the floor across from her.*
MOTHER *is reading a book while* MOLLY *thumbs through a teen magazine.*]

MOLLY. Mom! Look at this outfit! It's ridiculous! Can I go shopping?
MOTHER. Remind me again. 'Ridiculous' means good, right?
MOLLY. *[Sighs.]* You are such a tool, Mom. 'Ridiculous' means awesome, fabulous, beyond!
MOTHER. And 'tool' is a bad thing, right?
MOLLY. Well, not a bad thing exactly, but definitely a geek...or in your generation, *[Laughs.]*
'square'....yes, absolutely! You are 'square'. *[Beat.]* Can I?
MOTHER. Go shopping? Not for that outfit!
MOLLY. Why-eee?
MOTHER. Too provocative. Maybe when you're eighteen, not fourteen.
MOLLY. But, Mom, *[Whining.]* all the girls are wearing this.
MOTHER. Well, apparently not all the girls.

[Silence. Several beats as THEY *read.]*

MOLLY. Mom! Guess what?
MOTHER. Hmm?
MOLLY. Mom! Listen!

[MOTHER *puts* HER *book aside.]*

MOTHER. I'm listening, Molly.
MOLLY. Guess what!

MOTHER. *[This is an old game.]* How many guesses do I get?
MOLLY. *[Grins.]* One.
MOTHER. You bought a car?
MOLLY. *[Laughs.]* That is so lame. I don't even get my learner's permit for another two years.
MOTHER. Oh, well. I guess I lose. What's up?
MOLLY. Bethany is having a slumber party next weekend...*[Dramatic beat.]... and* she invited me!
MOTHER. Bethany and that crowd aren't your friends....
MOLLY. I know! That's what's so awesome about it! Outta the blue she walks up to me after English.
MOLLY. I was at my locker, and she walks up with Courtney and Melissa and asks me if I want to come. I can, can't I, Mom?
MOTHER. We'll have to see...
MOLLY. *[Interrupts.]* Mom! You have to say yes. Those girls have never, even said 'hi' to me much less invited me anywhere. I have to go.
MOTHER. I'll call Bethany's mother.
MOLLY. Moommm! You can't! Bethany will think I'm a baby.
MOTHER. I'm certain the other girls' mothers will be calling too. And I am sure that Bethany's Mom calls the parents if Bethany sleeps over.
MOLLY. But, Mom...
MOTHER. That's the only chance you have of going.
MOLLY. Okkaaay.
MOTHER. Is Mary Ellen invited too?
MOLLY. No. She told me, when we were on the bus, that Bethany hasn't said a word to her. She's really jealous that I get to go.
MOTHER. How does that make you feel? She's your best friend.
MOLLY. Jeez...Mom…
MOTHER. Language.
MOLLY. Jeepers, Mom. I can't help it if Bethany didn't invite Mary Ellen. I love her bunches but she is a tool, ya'know.
MOTHER. And you're not?
MOLLY. *[Smug.]* I guess not. Maybe it's the new haircut you gave me for my birthday.

*[**MOTHER** stares at **MOLLY**.]*

MOLLY. I don't know, okay?! I just know that one of the most ridiculous girls in school has invited me!
MOTHER. Before I call, I want you to think this through, Mols. Ask yourself why all the interest from Bethany and her group. Why now after snubbing you all through middle school. She must know you and Mary L' are best friends; why not invite her too?
MOLLY. Jeez...I mean..Jeepers! Mom! Do you have to make a federal case out of *everything?* This is so important and I have to go...I just have to!

MOTHER. All right. It's your decision. But, I want you to sleep on it. Tomorrow if you feel the same way, I'll call Bethany's mother.

[MOLLY rushes over to HER mother and hugs HER.]

MOLLY. You're the best!

Scene   2

Setting. The living room.

[**MOLLY** *sits on the floor.* **MOTHER** *is on the sofa with a cell phone on the table.*]

MOTHER. So you've decided?
MOLLY. Absolutely! Bethany and Melissa and Courtney are being so nice to me. They see me in the halls and say 'hello' and they're laughing and so friendly.
MOTHER. Okay then.

[**MOTHER** *dials her cell phone and waits for an answer.* **MOLLY**'s *eyes are glued on* **HER**.]

MOTHER. Hello...may I speak to Mrs. Pierson?...Oh, hello, this is Mrs. Albrecht calling...Molly's mother? Yes, how are you? *[Listens.]* I'm fine. Bethany has been so kind as to invite Molly to her slumber party this Saturday and I wanted to check with you about supervision...*[Listens. Laughs.]*...Yes, they are at that age. The 'family room'? Oh, you are. Well, that's just fine then. *[Listens.]* Yes, I'd be happy to... What time should I pick Molly up on Sunday? That'll be fine. I'll drop her off around five o'clock Saturday then. Thank you. *[She hangs up and turns to Molly.]*Both of Bethany's parents will be there. She has assured me that it's girls only and asked me to send some cupcakes. *[Beat.]* Well, that's it then. If you want to go, I guess you can.
MOLLY. *[Jumps up and sits on the sofa.]* You are the most ridiculous Mom in the whole world.

MOTHER. I hope you know what you're doing. Just be careful.
MOLLY. What should I wear? Do you know where my sleeping bag is? Will you make chocolate cupcakes?

Scene   3

Setting. The Pierson's family room. Loud punk rock blares. A disco-light flashes. Loud laughter and talking. There is smoke in the air.

> [*There are five other girls besides* **MOLLY** *and eight boys.* (Cast numbers can be adjusted.) **THEY** *are dancing and drinking alcohol.* **MOLLY** *stands to the side.*
> **BETHANY** *approaches.*]

BETHANY. [*Laughing and tipsy.*] Isn't this ridiculous Molly? Why aren't you dancing? Want me to get you a drink?
MOLLY. No thanks. I have a Coke.
BETHANY. Whas' the matter? Don't be shy.   Hey! Look, everyone! Our Molly-Dolly is scared!
MOLLY. [*Bravado.*] I'm not scared.
BETHANY. Who's gonna dance with Molly?
Danny, come teach our little Molly some dirty dancing.
MOLLY. That's okay, Bethany. I don't want to dance.
BETHANY. Come on, don't be such a wall flower.
MOLLY. Really, I'm fine. You go ahead.
BETHANY. You are such a loser!
MOLLY. I'm sorry.
BETHANY. Did you actually think that I liked you? A total tool? Don't look now, Molly-dolly, but you're the party favor! Everybody likes a good joke. Hey! Everybody! Who wants a party favor?

> [**MOLLY** *turns and runs from the room.*]

BETHANY. What a dweeb! Danny, my cup is empty.

[**BETHANY** *dives back into the dancing.*]

Scene   4

Setting.   Molly's living room. Later. Saturday night.

[**MOTHER** *sits on the sofa, feet up, reading a book.* **SHE** *stretches and yawns.*]

MOTHER. Time for bed. *[Beat.]* Who'd a thought the house would be so empty and quiet with Mol's gone? *[Rising.]* Who knew?

[**MOTHER's** *cell phone rings. Still at the party,* **MOLLY** *enters far down stage on* **HER** *cell phone.* **SHE** *is crying.*]

MOTHER. Hello?...who is this?... Molly! Is that you? Molly! What's wrong?
MOLLY. Mommy? It's awful here.
MOTHER. Mols, what's happened? Are you all right? Molly! You've got to stop crying and tell me where you are...are you okay!?
MOLLY. Mommy...can you come and get me? Please?
MOTHER. Yes, yes, of course. Where are you? Are you safe?
MOLLY. I'm...*[begins to cry again.]*...I'm hiding under the back porch at Bethany's house. Mommy, it was all a joke, a trick...they were laughing at me.
MOTHER. Its okay, Baby. Don't move. I'm coming.
MOLLY. Mom! Don't talk to Bethany's parents...PLEASE! Just come and get me. Promise.
MOTHER. Of course. I'm on my way...don't move.

[**MOTHER** *rises and rushes out of the room, still talking.*]

MOTHER. It's going to be okay, Mols. Just stay where you are...I'll be there in ten minutes. Just keep talking to me...
                    [**SHE** *exits.*]

Scene 5

Setting. The living room. An hour later.

[**MOLLY** *sits on the sofa, wrapped in a blanket drinking from a mug.* **MOTHER** *is sitting in a chair across from her.*]

MOTHER. Do you want to talk about it?
MOLLY. I guess.
MOTHER. We don't have to. Finish your hot chocolate and we'll go to bed. Things always look better in the morning.
MOLLY. Why do you always say that?
MOTHER. Because it's true. Because your wise, old mother has found that sleeping on something usually puts it in perspective.
MOLLY. Well, it's not true this time. My life is over. We'll have to move away. I can never go back to that school again.
MOTHER. That's why I think we should sleep on it. But, it's your decision; if you want to talk about it
tonight...
MOLLY. I do want to...I don't know if I'll ever sleep again. It was so awful, Mom.

[**MOTHER** *rises and crosses to the sofa.* **SHE** *sits on the opposite end and puts* **MOLLY**'s *feet in* **HER** *lap.*]

MOTHER. Your feet are like ice.

MOLLY. It's okay.

*[**MOTHER** tucks the end of the blanket around **MOLLY**'s feet.]*

MOTHER. Where were Bethany's parents, Mols?
MOLLY. They were there earlier. They came down and said 'hello' to all of us, before the boys got there.
MOTHER. Boys! But...
MOLLY. But I never saw them again.
MOTHER. Was there alcohol?
MOLLY. Yes, but I didn't want any. Then Bethany said I was a party favor...
MOTHER. Oh, honey...

*[**MOLLY** continues as if **SHE** had not spoken.]*

MOLLY. I was a joke...they were drinking punch and acting silly. The boys were acting weird. Grabbing the girls and dirty dancing....Bethany and Danny were kissing and...
MOTHER. Its okay, Mols. Take your time. It's over now and you're safe.
MOLLY. Anyway, I was just standing by the wall, watching. And Bethany...*[Beat.]*... Bethany comes over to me and asks me if I'm having a good time. She tells the boys that someone needs to dance with 'Molly-Dolly'...that's what she called me. That and 'party favor'. I'm not sure what that means but it didn't sound good.
MOTHER. Oh, honey, I'm sorry...
MOLLY. That's when I ran away. I was so scared, Mom. Bethany and Courtney and the rest of them don't like me....I was just a joke to them. And then I ran... like a baby.
MOTHER. The joke's on them, Mols. You acted with self-respect. You chose not to drink, you didn't do foolish things that you knew were wrong. I'm proud of you.
MOLLY. I'm not very good in the decision-making department. Mary Ellen tried to tell me...you tried to tell me. Going to that party was one, big, fat, BAD decision.
MOTHER. Now, hold on a minute. Maybe it was not the best idea, going to that party, but let's look at the great decisions you did make. You decided not to drink, not to get involved with those boys, not let Bethany and her friends pressure you into things that were wrong. You made another good decision by getting out of there and finding a safe place. And the best decision of all, you called me!
MOLLY. Yeah, I guess.
MOTHER. Honey, life is full of decision making. Sometimes we get it right, sometimes not so much...
MOLLY. Have you made some bad ones?

*[**MOTHER** laughs derisively.]*

MOTHER. Oh, yeah, I've made my share. But the trick is to make more good decisions than bad. And learn from the bad ones that we make.

MOLLY. You're my BFF you know that, Mom?

MOTHER. Thanks! I think.

CURTAIN

BOBBY AND ELEANORA

by

Trisha Sugarek

<u>CAST OF CHARACTERS</u>

ELEANORA - An elderly lady in her eighties. She appears to be bed ridden and ill. She has a timeless beauty.

BOBBY - A handsome man in his late thirties. He is dashing and suave. He and Eleanora were lovers and married forty years ago.

ELEANORA - At age thirty.

Production Notes: Low lighting with spots should be used as younger Eleanor needs to enter and get into the bed unnoticed.

A chair can replace the bed.

Scene 1

Setting. A darkened bedroom. A spot comes up on a elderly woman lying in the bed.

*[***ELEANORA*** *sits bold upright, taking a panicky gasp.]*

ELEANORA. OH! How vivid! I could have swore...but no...that's not possible. *[Scoffs.]* Oh, Eleanora, you are becoming a daffy old woman. If only it were true...*[Sighing.]* No, nothing can bring him back.

[In the shadows, a man speaks. ***BOBBY*** *is handsome and dressed formally.]*

BOBBY. Eleanora...
ELEANORA. Who's there?
BOBBY. Ellie, I'm disappointed. Don't you know me?
ELEANORA. Bobby? But what? How? .....where did you come from? I thought I was dreaming...
BOBBY. Then we are both dreaming, my darling. I have dreamed of this moment for decades.
ELEANORA. If this is a dream, I hope I never wake up.

*[***BOBBY*** *walks to the side of the bed. *or chair.* ***HE*** *holds out his hands.]*

BOBBY. Come, my love, walk with me.
ELEANORA. I can't, Bobby. I've been bedridden for two years now.
BOBBY. Yes, you can. Trust me.

[Tentatively ***ELEANORA*** *takes* ***HIS*** *hands and rises.* ***SHE*** *pauses.]*

ELEANORA. I'm afraid.
BOBBY. With me? Have I ever let you down?
ELEANORA. Yes.

BOBBY. *[Shocked.]* When?

ELEANORA. When you died.

BOBBY. Oh, yes. I'm sorry for that. I didn't get a vote, my darling. I would never have left you. But, it was my time. *[Beat.]* I've never been very far away. Didn't you know?

ELEANORA. Yes...but I thought it was just an old fool's fancy. I...I felt you sometimes but...

BOBBY. You should have trusted your feelings, Ellie. Didn't I always tell you to?

ELEANORA. Yes, my love. But, as the years went by and I got old and sick, I was so frightened that I would become a batty, old crone. Talking to myself or even worse, talking to people who weren't there.....Oh! I'm standing.

BOBBY. Yes, and you can walk if you wish. Come.

[BOBBY places HER hand in the crook of his arm. ELEANORA takes a few tentative steps. In the dark, at the bed, a YOUNGER ELEANOR enters and is hidden under the covers. SHE is dressed in the same night dress.]

ELEANORA. How is this possible? I haven't been able to use my legs for a long time. The doctors wanted to....

BOBBY. *[Finishes her sentence.]* Amputate. Yes, I know. I stopped them.

ELEANORA. You? But how?

BOBBY. I didn't want them to start cutting pieces off of you. You were in no danger so why take your legs?

ELEANORA. How am I able to walk?

BOBBY. This is a special time for just the two of us. You can walk, run, dance....would you like to dance with me, Ellie?

ELEANORA. Oh, yes, more than anything in this world.

[BOBBY takes her into his arms as waltz music plays very softly. Several beats of dancing. ELEANORA begins to weep.]

BOBBY. My darling love, what's wrong?

ELEANORA. Nothing. I'm just so happy. I never danced again, not since you went away. I never thought to waltz again.

[BOBBY stops dancing.]

ELEANORA. Kiss me.

BOBBY. No.

ELEANORA. No? But why? *[Beat.]* You don't love me anymore.

BOBBY. I love you with all my heart. It's just not time yet.

ELEANORA. Whatever do you mean?

BOBBY. Soon. Will you trust me?

ELEANORA. With my life. *[Beat.]* So....you're dead, Bobby?
BOBBY. Yes.
 ELEANORA. Why aren't you older?....my age?
BOBBY. Because when you die, my sweet, you get to choose what age to be.
ELEANORA. Really?
BOBBY. Yes, really.
ELEANORA. Do you see...others...that have gone...died?
BOBBY. Only if you wish it.

> *[**BOBBY** kisses **ELEANORA** on the cheek.]*

 BOBBY. It's hard to understand during our mortal time...when you pass on there are no recriminations, no blame, no guilt, no anger.   It all passes away.
ELEANORA. Did you come to me in a dream after you died?
BOBBY. Ah, you remember that, do you? Yes, I came to say goodbye. And to hold you one last time. Do you remember that too?
ELEANORA. *[Whispers.]*   Yes, I remember.
BOBBY. You were always the love of my life. Why did you leave me?
ELEANORA. Why, indeed? Because I was a stupid, stupid girl. Always looking for that perfect man, that perfect love.
BOBBY. When all the time, you were with your perfect love. Certainly not a perfect man, but no one could have loved you more. Did he exist, that perfect man?
ELEANORA. No.
BOBBY. Were you happy?
ELEANORA. Sometimes.
BOBBY. I'm sorry.
ELEANORA. It doesn't matter anymore. You're here. *[Beat.]*   Bobby?
BOBBY. Yes, darling....
ELEANORA. When will you kiss me?
BOBBY. It's time now. Come. Come back to bed.

> *[**BOBBY** walks **HER** back to the side of the bed. Before **BOBBY** helps the elder* ***ELEANORA*** *back into the bed,* **HE** *kisses her mouth sweetly.* **HE** *then lays her on the bed and covers* **HER**.]*

ELEANORA. Bobby, don't leave me. Please.
BOBBY. I will be right here, my love. Sleep now. When you awake, we'll go on a trip like we used to do.

[BOBBY continues smoothing her hair, kissing her face, speaking to her in soft, loving   words.]

BOBBY. Remember our trip to Catalina Island, Ellie?   It was our fifth wedding anniversary.   We met that gypsy woman on the beach.   She had a parrot and that awful monkey with her.   *[HE laughs.]*   That monkey was such a terror.   The gypsy woman was so beautiful and you were jealous.   You wouldn't believe that I had eyes only for you....and the couple we met in the cafe later that afternoon. They lived on their boat and we swam out to have cocktails with them....Ellie?

*[**ELEANORA** appears to be in a deep sleep, but in fact has died.]*

...Yes, sleep, my love....for that's really all that death is....

*[As **BOBBY** kisses **HER** forehead and then straightens, the **YOUNGER ELEANORA** slowly rises from the other side of the bed. **BOBBY** and **SHE** join hands over the body of the elder Eleanor. **THEY** walk simultaneously down either side of the bed and meet at the foot.]*

ELEANORA. Bobby!   What took you so long?   I've been waiting and waiting.
BOBBY. Am I so very late?
ELEANOR. It seems like I have been waiting a life time for you.
BOBBY. What's one life time when we have all eternity together?   I love you, Ellie, only you.

CURTAIN

LOVE NEVER LEAVES BRUISES

by

Trisha Sugarek

CAST of CHARACTERS

Megan - 15, the girl friend

Tommy - 17, the boy friend

Pam - Megan's mother

Author's Note: These staggering statistics inspired me to write a play addressing this topic, with the hope that it might help stop the violence. About one in three high school students have been or will be involved in an abusive relationship.

Forty percent of teenage girls ages 14 to 17 say they know someone their age that has been hit or beaten by a boyfriend. A survey of 500 young women, ages 15 to 24, found that 60 percent were currently involved in an ongoing abusive relationship and all participants had experienced violence in a dating relationship.

For help and more information visit: www.loveisrespect.org

Scene 1

Setting.   A neutral place at school. A brick wall, under the stadium stands, or outside the locker room.

[**TOMMY** *has* **MEGAN** *by the arm.* **HE** *suddenly pushes* **HER** *hard up against a wall.*]

TOMMY. You were flirting with him!
MEGAN. No, Tommy, I wasn't.
TOMMY. Don't lie to me, Megan. I saw you.
MEGAN. No, I promise.
TOMMY. You're such a tramp. I don't know why I go with you.
MEGAN. Tommy, he's my lab partner. I was just kidding around with him about our experiment exploding in class today.....
TOMMY. Bull crap. I saw you batting your eyes at him.

[**TOMMY** *grabs* **HER** *by the shoulders and slams* **HER** *against the wall again.*]

TOMMY. Did he ask you out, huh? Did you say yes?
MEGAN. No. Cut it out. You're hurting me.
TOMMY. *[Raising a clinched fist.]* I'll hurt you a lot worse if you flirt with another guy. You belong to me.
MEGAN. I know, I know. But, I wasn't flirting.
TOMMY. Stop saying you weren't.... I saw you with my own eyes.

[**TOMMY** *puts* **HIS** *hand around* **MEGAN** *'s throat.*]

TOMMY. You're a b......
VOICE [Off.] Hey! You kids. Break it up! You're not supposed to be here. Where are your passes?

*[**MEGAN** breaks free and runs off. **TOMMY** runs off the other way.]*

Scene 2

Setting. Megan's living room.

> [**PAM, MEGAN's** *mother sits on the sofa. A door slams.* **MEGAN** *enters.* **SHE** *throws* **HER** *backpack down and flops into a chair.*

PAM. Don't slam the door please.

 MEGAN. Goodd! School is so lame.

PAM. Language! *[Beat.]* So, why is school lame today?

MEGAN. Lunch was gross, our lab experiment exploded and we have a re-do, and Tommy's acting all weird.

PAM.*[Using the same cadence.]* You took your lunch. You have to get a decent grade in chemistry. And.... *[Picking up on the last complaint.]* Weird, how?

MEGAN. I don't know. He gets all jealous and everything.

PAM. You're crazy about him. Why would he be jealous?

MEGAN. Charlie and I were laughing in the hall after chemistry. About our lab assignment shooting green slime on the ceiling.....

PAM. 'Onto' the ceiling....

MEGAN. Whatever. Green slime onto the ceiling and Tommy came up and got all mad, gave Charlie the evil eye and stormed off. *[Beat.]* I wasn't doing anything!

PAM. Hormones. Tommy will get over it.

MEGAN. I'm not speaking to him until he says he's sorry. *[Beat.]* Have we got any food? I've got tons of homework.

PAM. I believe we keep that in the kitchen.

> [**THEY** *laugh together.* **MEGAN** *exits.]*

Scene 3

Setting. The living room. The next afternoon.

> *[PAM is pacing while **SHE** waits for **MEGAN** to return from school. A door slams.*
> ***MEGAN** enters, drops **HER** backpack on the floor.]*

MEGAN. I'm starved. Anything to eat in the house?

> [**PAM** *is silent.* **MEGAN** *notices.]*

What? *[Beat.]* What's wrong?
PAM. *[Sits on the sofa.]* Sit. We need to talk.
MEGAN. *[Sighs.]* Whad' I do now?
PAM. I don't know that you did anything. *[Beat.]* I got a call from the school this morning.
MEGAN. Jeezch! I'm going to do the lab work over, okay?
PAM. It isn't about your lab work. Mrs. Henderson called regarding what she called, 'a disturbing event'. She told me that school security found you and Tommy outside the gym, during classes, alone. No passes. Security told her that when he called out to you kids, you ran off like, let's see what were her exact words? Oh, yes, 'you ran off like a scalded cat.' Security told Mrs. Henderson that it appeared that you and Tommy were arguing.

> *[**MEGAN** is silent.]*

PAM. Well? Is it true? Do you have anything to say? *[Silence.]* Okay. You want to play it that way? You're grounded until you tell me what happened.
MEGAN. Moomm! Nothing happened. I already told you Tommy was jealous about the Charlie thing and we were talking about it between classes. Nothing happened! I ran 'cause I was late for class.

*[MEGAN rises and starts to leave. **PAM** rises and quickly crosses to **HER**. **PAM** takes her by the shoulders. **MEGAN** flinches. **SHE** is still sore from **TOMMY**'s assault.]*

PAM. Meggie, I just want you....What's wrong? Are you hurt?
MEGAN. *[Pulls away from her mother.]* No! No!
PAM. But you flinched. Let me see your arm.
MEGAN. Nothing's wrong with my arm.
PAM. Then you don't have any reason not to show it to me.

*[**MEGAN** sighs and rolls up **HER** sleeve. There are dark bruises on **HER** upper arm.]*

PAM. What in the world! What happened?
MEGAN. I ran into a door running for my English class all right? Shish, leave me alone, why don'cha.

*[**MEGAN** runs off.]*

 PAM. Megan! You come back here.

Scene 4

Setting. At school. Lunch break.

   [TOMMY is sitting with HIS arm loosely around MEGAN's shoulders.]

MEGAN. I love you, you know that, right?
TOMMY. Sure.
MEGAN. So, we're cool, right?
TOMMY. Sure, Babe.
MEGAN. You got football practice after school?
TOMMY. Why do you want to know? So you can sneak off and meet that guy?
MEGAN. *[Sighs.]* No....I was just asking, okay?
TOMMY. Yeah, I guess. Did you get a new lab partner like I told you?
MEGAN. Tommy, I asked, I really did. Ms. Allen said lab partners are assigned for the semester.....no switching.
VOICE Off. Hey! Megan. See ya in chemistry!

   [MEGAN gives CHARLIE a half-hearted wave.]

TOMMY. What're ya waving to that geek for? *[Beat.]* You like him! I can tell.
MEGAN. Tommy, why do you have to be so weird? Huh? I don't like Charlie that way. I love you.
 TOMMY. What'd you call me? Weird? Did my ears hear you right? Weird? You're dating a football star, you stupid little tramp.

MEGAN. I'm sorry, I didn't mean anything by it. But, why do you have to be all jealous and mad and everything? Sometimes you act all crazy...

    *[***TOMMY*** *punches* **HER** *in the face.* **MEGAN** *doubles over and begins to cry.]*

TOMMY. *You* make me crazy.... why ya gotta make me do things....why ya gotta make me so mad?

    *[***MEGAN*** *jumps up and runs off.]*

TOMMY. Come back here. Meg! I love you. I'm sorry.

Scene 5

Setting. The living room. That afternoon.

[MEGAN sits on the sofa. HER homework is spread on the coffee table. SHE wears a baseball cap with the bill low over HER eyes. A door closes Off. PAM enters wearing work clothes.]

PAM. Hey, Baby girl? How was school?

[MEGAN keeps HER head down and continues writing.]

MEGAN. Fine.
PAM. Fine? No complaints? *[Laughs.]* Are you sick or something?

[MEGAN slams HER book shut and piling all her homework into HER arms, SHE rises and starts to leave. As SHE passes Pam, head down, PAM lifts the cap off MEGAN's head.]

PAM. No hats on in the house.

[MEGAN makes a grab for the cap and misses.]

MEGAN. Mom!
PAM. Hey! What's with all the makeup? Is it that time of the month for zits?

[PAM takes a closer look. SHE gently takes MEGAN's chin in her hand and moves MEGAN's face up into the light.]

PAM. Meggie, what's wrong with your eye? IS THAT A BRUISE!?

[PAM starts to rub off the makeup with HER thumb.]

MEGAN. Ooowww! That hurts! Cut it out!
PAM. I'm sorry. *[Beat.]* Go in the kitchen and wash your face, Megan. I'll be waiting here.

[PAM wearily sits on the sofa. A few moments later MEGAN enters. SHE has the beginnings of a black eye. SHE has the cap back on.]

PAM. Sit here with me, honey. *[Megan sits. Pam gently takes the cap off and looks at Megan's eye carefully.]* My God! What happened?
MEGAN. Nothing.
PAM. Meggie, I'm not mad at you. You can tell me. What happened?
MEGAN. Nothing! It happened at soccer practice, okay?

[PAM knows MEGAN is lying.]

PAM. I can call the school and speak with your coach, you know.
MEGAN. No! Don't do that!
PAM. Bruises on your arm. Now this? *[Beat.]* Did Tommy do this to you?
MEGAN. *[Scared. Begins to cry.]* NO!
PAM. Baby, you can tell me. Haven't we always told each other everything? *[Not a question.]* Tommy did this.
MEGAN. He didn't mean to, Mom, honest.
PAM. Oh my Gosh! Tommy hit you?
MEGAN. He loves me, Mom. It's just that he gets jealous. He didn't mean to do it. He's always so sorry after. I say the wrong thing and then he....
 PAM. Meggie, honey, I don't care what you might have said. There's no reason on earth a guy has the right to hurt you? Don't you know that? How long has this been going on?
MEGAN. Just a month or two.
PAM. *[Shocked.]* 'Just a month or two'.....

MEGAN. Tommy used to get mad and would call me names but he never hit me...well, this one time he did shove me. But, he's so sorry after he cools down and he loves me, Mom. Then Ms. Allen assigned me and Charlie as lab partners and Tommy got all weird about it.

PAM. So, Mrs. Henderson's call the other day? You and Tommy....?

MEGAN. We were just arguing and Tommy grabbed me by the throat....

PAM. What!?

MEGAN. So I wouldn't leave, Mom. And then security caught us...

*[**PAM** realizes that **MEGAN** has been wearing turtle necks.]*

PAM. Let me see.

MOLLY. It's nothing, Mom.

PAM. Let me see, Megan.

*[**MEGAN** pulls down **HER** collar. **PAM** can see old and new bruises. **SHE** gasps.]*

MEGAN. Please, Mom. I love him. He loves me. Other girls' boyfriends get rough with them. It's no big deal.

PAM. No big deal? This is domestic violence. Part of 'love' is respect, Megan. Love never hurts. Haven't I always told you that if you respect yourself, everyone else will too? If Tommy is putting his hands on you, he doesn't love or respect you.

MEGAN. But, I love him. Don't make me break up with him. *[Pleading.]* Please.

PAM. Oh! You are so going to break up with him! Actually, I'm going to break up with him for you. That boy is never coming near you again.

MEGAN. Mom! You can't!

PAM. Meggie, this is the part where being the Mom is no fun. I know you're probably not going to understand this but you are in serious danger. If you continue dating Tommy it will only get worse. He could hurt you very badly or even kill you.

MEGAN. *[Indignant.]* Tommy would never...

PAM. This is what we are going to do. First, we're going to go on line and look it up. There's got to be a way to Google dating violence. You don't have to take my word for it. Google it and see what other teens are saying. Next I'm calling your counselor at school and setting up a meeting with her, Tommy and Tommy's parents.

MEGAN. Mom! You wouldn't!

PAM. Oh, yes, I would and shall. You won't be there. If Tommy's parents agree to counseling for Tommy, I won't press charges.

MEGAN. You can't! I'll die of embarrassment. I'll never be able to show my face again.

PAM. Who's going to know? I'm certain Tommy won't tell anyone. You and I won't. So how are your friends going to find out?

MEGAN. They'll know. Can't we just forget about it? I promise I won't see Tommy again. Can we, Mom, please?

PAM. And what if a year from now you hear that Tommy has hurt or killed some other girl, Megan? How would you feel then about the fact that you didn't do anything to help Tommy?

MEGAN. You're impossible! I'm never going to tell you anything *ever* again!

[**MEGAN** *rises and runs from the room.*]

Scene 6

Setting. Two weeks later. The living room.

[PAM sits on the sofa reading the newspaper. A door slams Off. **MEGAN** *enters.]*

MEGAN. Hi Mom!
PAM. Hi. *[Beat.]* Are you speaking to me again?
MEGAN. *[Sheepish.] Yeah.* Can I have a snack before I start my homework?
PAM. There's warm cookies on the counter. Drink a glass of milk. No Coke.
MEGAN. Okay. Thanks.

*[***MEGAN*** *starts to exit.* **SHE** *turns back.]*

MEGAN. Mom?
PAM. Hmm?
MEGAN. I love you. You know that, right?

*[***PAM*** *lowers the paper and looks at* **MEGAN**.*]*

PAM. What brought this on? I thought you hated me.
MEGAN. Tommy transferred to another school. I didn't realize until he was gone how stressed I was dating him. Now I know what you mean when you say, walking on egg shells. And Charlie asked me to go to the game with him Friday night. Anyway... I just wanted to say thank you and let you know that I love you.

[As **MEGAN** *exits.]*

PAM. I love you too, kiddo.

CURTAIN

The Waltz

by

Trisha Sugarek

CAST OF CHARACTERS

Connie - An eighteen year old tomboy dressed in a gown.

John - A dashing young bachelor.

Violet's voice Off - Connie's sister

Author's Note: this love story is inspired by a true tale about my favorite Aunt and her underpants.

Scene 1

Setting. 1920. A ballroom. A company dinner dance.

[**CONNIE***, barely eighteen and lovely in a coltish way, stands off to the side while the music plays. A new waltz is starting. A handsome young man approaches.]*

JOHN. Excuse me, Miss Guyer?
CONNIE. Yes?
JOHN. I'm John Gibbons and....Forgive me, I know we haven't been introduced but I'm a friend of Bill Murphy's and....well....I....with this crush tonight, I can't get him over here to introduce us. Anyway, I was wondering if you....
CONNIE. *[Nervous.]* Yes?
JOHN......would like to dance?
CONNIE. Well, since you're a friend of Bill's....I suppose it'll be all right....Yes! I would love to dance, Mr. Gibbons.

[*The waltz music has begun.* **JOHN** *takes* **CONNIE** *into his arms and* **THEY** *begin to dance.]*

JOHN. Bill says you work for his father.
CONNIE. Yes, I'm in the secretarial pool. May I ask? What is it that you do, Mr. Gibbons?
JOHN. I'm an attorney. I work at the firm that represents Bill's father's company.
CONNIE. Oh. How nice. *[Beat.]* It's a lovely party, don't you think?
JOHN. A little too stiff for my taste, if you'll forgive me for saying so, Miss Guyer.

CONNIE. Oh, no, there's nothing to forgive. It's pretty snooty for my taste too. But the music's very nice. I love to waltz, don't you?

JOHN. Not until tonight. *[Beat.]* With you, Miss Guyer?....I adore the waltz. *[Beat.]* Have you lived in Seattle your whole life?

CONNIE. Oh, no. I was raised in a little town outside of Olympia.

JOHN. Ah, our state capital. I have visited Olympia several times. My firm sometimes has a case that reaches the Supreme Court.   What's the name of your 'little town'?

CONNIE. You've never heard of it. Tumwater.

JOHN. *[HE grins.]* You're right, I never have. Is your family still there?

CONNIE. *[Laughs.]* Oh, yes.

JOHN. What's so funny about that?

CONNIE. When people ask about my 'family', they have no idea what they are getting in to.

JOHN. Intriguing.....give me details.

CONNIE. Well to start with....I have a lot of brothers and sisters.

JOHN. Really? I have two of each myself. Five kids. What a mob growing up.

CONNIE. Five? A mere pittance. Nothing remarkable in five....

JOHN. All right, Miss Guyer....out do me if you can.

CONNIE. Thirteen!

[JOHN stops dancing and stares at HER.]

JOHN. What?

CONNIE. Shall we continue? People are having to dance around us.

[THEY begin to dance again.]

JOHN. Oh, yes, of course. Did I hear you correctly? You did say 'thirteen'?

CONNIE. Six sisters and seven brothers.

JOHN. *[In awe.]* Thirteen.

CONNIE. *[Laughing.]* Your mouth is open, Mr. Gibbons.

JOHN. *[Snaps it shut.]* Forgive me. I am stunned. *[Beat.]* Are all of the girls as lovely as you?

CONNIE. Oh, no, Mr. Gibbons, I am considered the ugly one....

JOHN. Then the other sisters must resemble Diana and Venus if they are more beautiful than you, Miss Guyer.

CONNIE. *[Blushing.]* Please, you're embarrassing me.

JOHN. I apologize. It's just that your eyes are so lovely. Your gown matches them perfectly. And may I tell you a secret?

CONNIE. Yes.

JOHN. I was terrified that I wouldn't get an introduction and some other man would sweep you into a waltz and you would be lost to me forever.

[JOHN twirls HER around.]

CONNIE. Mr. Gibbons, please, we've just met.

JOHN. I am sorry. Let me find a safer subject. [Beat.] Tell me, what does your father do?

CONNIE. [Proud of her father.] He's a woodsman.

JOHN. Really? I'm not sure what that means.

CONNIE. He works in the forest. He's hired by people to cut trees and harvest the best wood. But he is very good at conservation and advises the owners of the trees about seeding and leaving stands of trees to propagate new growth....

[JOHN is grinning at HER enthusiasm. CONNIE looks up and sees his grin.]

CONNIE. Oh! I am sorry. I tend to go on and on about things....

[The orchestra begins a second waltz. JOHN and CONNIE continue to dance, oblivious to everything.]

JOHN. Don't be. I find you thoroughly charming. You love your father very much. [Beat.] And your mother?

CONNIE. She's the best. I admire her so much. She's strong, witty, beautiful and wise. [Beat.] There I go again....I promise, I don't usually talk this much....you are just so easy to talk with, Mr. Gibbons.

JOHN. Would you even consider calling me John? I know that we've just met. It's probably too soon. I shouldn't have asked...

CONNIE. [Interrupts him.] I would love to call you John...and you must call me Connie...John.

JOHN. You don't think me too bold? I wouldn't offend you for the world.

CONNIE. Not at all. Mama always tells me that I'm too bold.

JOHN. Well! Shall we be bold together?

CONNIE. [Laughing up at him.] Yes, yes!

CONNIE. Oh, stop, stop, I'm going to fall down....

JOHN. And I'm going to fall in love....

CONNIE. Oh, John, you mustn't. It's too soon.

JOHN. I know but I can't help it. You are so refreshingly honest, Connie. So genuine. The young ladies I meet are lovely people, I'm sure....but....well...they all seem to have this calculating gleam in their eye...and their Mamas... [Laughing.] ...make me want to run for the hills.

CONNIE. Oh dear. Why?

JOHN. I'm what's known as an 'eligible bachelor'. Very eligible, they tell me.

CONNIE. Oh, I see.

JOHN. No, you don't *see*. Please don't look like that. I don't want to be up on the marriage block, as my fraternity brothers say. I don't want a bunch of greedy mothers arranging a marriage between me and one of their daughters.

CONNIE. What does your mother say about that?

JOHN. Oh, she knows me too well to try to arrange anything. She's great! She's always let me make my own decisions. My Dad's a doctor and she was hoping that I would follow in his footsteps, so to speak. But, the first time I saw a court room there was no turning back for me.

CONNIE. When was that?

JOHN. When I was twelve. My Dad was a expert witness in a trial and he thought he'd take me along so I could see how cut-throat lawyers can be. Boy, did it back fire on Dad. *[Laughing.]* Talk about love at first sight. *[HE gives her a meaningful look.]*   Say, twice in one life time. I've set a record.

> *[**CONNIE** doesn't speak. **SHE** gazes into his eyes.]*

JOHN. I want to see you again....soon. May I?

CONNIE. Yes...oh, yes.

JOHN. When?

CONNIE. I don't know... next weekend?

JOHN. Oh, don't torture me...next weekend? That's too long.

CONNIE. John, you do know that we are being very improper, don't you?   You should meet my parents. But, they live four hours away, and oh, it's all so confusing.

JOHN. If you want me to meet your parents before we go out, I'll drive down to your little town of Tumwater. Don't you know that's the least I would do for you.

JOHN. I want to do so much more...

CONNIE. You may call me this coming week and we'll arrange....

> *[Suddenly **CONNIE** stumbles....then stumbles again.]*

JOHN. Connie, are you all right?   What's wrong?

> *[**CONNIE** has lost all beat with the music and stops dancing. **SHE** feels something wrapped around her ankles. Looks down and sees that **HER** drawers have fallen down around her ankles. **SHE** looks up at **JOHN** mortified. **JOHN** is looking down and sees the same thing.]*

JOHN. Step out of them. Connie, step out of them!

CONNIE.   Let me go, Mr. Gibbons. I am so sorry....Please! Just let me go.

JOHN. Connie, do as I say. Step out of them.

> *[***CONNIE*** *steps out of the offending underwear. In one quick motion* ***JOHN*** *bends down and scoops them up. Without a pause,* ***HE*** *puts them in* ***HIS*** *jacket pocket and then continues to waltz.* ***HE*** *dances around until* ***HE*** *reaches the side of the dance floor nearest the Restrooms.]*

JOHN. There. We made it with no one the wiser. I believe we will find the ladies room right over there. I'll wait right here until you have made the necessary repairs.

CONNIE. No, please, John, don't wait for me. I'm going home.

> *[***SHE*** *puts out* ***HER*** *hand and* ***JOHN*** *gives* ***HER*** *the drawers.]*

 It was a pleasure to meet you.

JOHN. Connie, please, this doesn't change anything.

CONNIE. Oh, yes, it changes EVERYTHING!

JOHN. Changes what I see in your eyes? Changes what I feel? A little scrap of cloth?

CONNIE. Yes...'a little scrap of cloth'. *[Heartbroken.]* Goodbye....John.

> *[***CONNIE*** *exits into the ladies room leaving* ***JOHN*** *standing there, dumfounded.]*

Scene 2

Setting. Connie's home. The kitchen. The next morning.

[The phone is ringing. Off. **CONNIE** *is the only one in the kitchen.]*

VIOLET. *[Off.]* I'll get it! *[Mumbling.]* Connie! It's for you.
CONNIE. *[Turns toward her sister's voice.]* Who is it?
VIOLET. *[Off.]* Some guy.
CONNIE. Can you act like a lady for once and ask for a name?
VIOLET. *[Mumbling. Yells to her sister.]* Some guy named John. John Ribbons?
CONNIE. *[Gasps.]* Oh, my stars! John.

[CONNIE exits for a beat and comes back with a phone to her ear.]

CONNIE. Hello?

CURTAIN

THE *PERFUME* BOTTLE

by

Trisha Sugarek

CAST OF CHARACTERS

Violet - A nine year old. She is the younger
sister of Ivah.

Ivah - An eleven year old, she is the prankster of the family.

Widow Pruitt - A mean old lady who gets the girls into trouble.

Author's note: Another true story about my mother and her outrageous sisters.

Scene 1

Setting. The woods behind their farm house.

[**VIOLET** *and* **IVAH** *are cutting branches from a bush.]*

VIOLET. I hate the widow Pruitt!
IVAH. She's a big ole tattle tale!
VIOLET. She's just a big baby! Can't she take a joke?

[**THEY** *continue to chop away at the bush.* **IVAH** *starts to giggle.]*

IVAH. How were we to know that she was in the outhouse when we tipped it over?
VIOLET. Then she had to go and tell Mama.
IVAH. It was an accident. It's not fair. Eddie and Earl didn't get caught. How could they think that we could tip it over by ourselves?
VIOLET. *[Teary.]* And now we're gonna get a switchin'...
IVAH. Oh, now Vi, it's not so bad. You know Mama thinks the biggest part of our punishment is pickin' out the switch she's gonna use on us. She never hits very hard....I hardly feel it.
VIOLET. *[Giggling and sniffling at the same time.]* I know. Mama's such a softy. When she gets upset with me and all kinda' hurt acting; well it's worse than any ole' switching...
IVAH. Well, we're gonna get ole lady Pruitt back....but good!
VIOLET. Oooh. *[Gleefully.]* What're we gonna do, Ivah?
IVAH. You'll see. When's Mama cookin' ham hocks and navy beans next?
VIOLET. Saturday night, why?
IVAH. *[Sagely.]* You'll see. Come on... we gotta get our saved up money and get down to the Five N' Dime before Mr. Golden closes.
VIOLET. Why?
IVAH. You'll see....

[THEY exit.   They re-enter from across the stage.]

VIOLET. Ivy... *[HER nickname for Ivah.]*
IVAH. Don't call me Ivy, I'm not a plant!
VIOLET. Why do we have to use my favorite hair ribbons? I've only worn them once.
IVAH. 'Cause this gift is for the widow Pruitt and it's gotta be perfect...did you bring the bottle?
VIOLET. Yes...and the old cork outta Pa's work bench.
IVAH. And the stationary and envelope?
VIOLET. *[Pulling them out of HER pocket.]* Do you think Mama will notice I took these? They're her best.
IVAH. No. *[Taking the cork from Violet.]* Good work, little sister.
VIOLET. Don't call me 'little'. I'm almost ten and I'm taller than you.
IVAH. Okay, okay...now give me the bottle and stand back!

[IVAH goes behind a bush or tree and there is the sound of farting. VIOLET begins to gasp and giggle and scream.]

VIOLET. Oh, oh, stop, Ivy! I can smell you clear out here! My eyes are watering.
IVAH. *[Giggling.]*   I told you to stand back. It's not my fault, Mama's beans always does this to me.
VIOLET. But Mama says that she cooks them upside down so we'll belch instead of.... *[Beat.]* well, you know...
IVAH. Fart? She just says that so we'll eat 'em.

[VIOLET giggles. IVAH comes out from where SHE has hidden, smoothing down her skirt.]

Now, where's that ribbon?
VIOLET. Right here.
IVAH. *[Working as SHE talks.]*   Now, we'll tie this beautiful bow around the top, like this....and then write the message on the stationary....let's see, what should it say?
VIOLET. Why do you get to write it? I want to *do* something.
IVAH. Because I have beautiful handwriting....everyone says so.
VIOLET. *[Whines.]* But, you get to do everything....what do *I* get to do?
IVAH. Oh, for goodness sakes, Vi, we're using your ribbons, aren't we? *[Beat.]* Oh, all right. You decide what we should say.
VIOLET. Let's see..'A special something for the big, ole, fat, tattletale'.
IVAH. *[Sarcastic.]* Oh that's great...should we sign it too, 'Love, Ivah and Violet Guyer' while we're at it?
VIOLET. We can't do that, Ivy! Then Mama will find out.... *[Finally gets it.]*   Oh...

IVAH. It's gotta be a message....like from a gentleman caller...less 'see...what would Rudolf Valentino say to Claire Bow?

VIOLET. *[Giggling with delight.]* 'I love you....I can't live without you....I'll die without you'..

[*SHE collapses into more giggles.*]

IVAH. I know. 'From a secret admirer...who worships you from afar'.

VIOLET. Oooo....that's good.   Write that.

[*IVAH turns VIOLET around and uses her back to write the message.*]

IVAH. *[Aloud.]* 'From a....secret admirer... who....worships you....from afar'... there! *[Shows Violet the paper.]* Some of my best penmanship, if I do say so.

VIOLET. That's really pretty, Ivy. Now what?

IVAH. The method of delivery. *[Beat.]* Mama would hear us if we snuck out after bedtime so that's no good. I know. Early morning, before anyone is up, I'll have a nature call and pretend to go out to the wash shed. Then I'll run over to the widow Pruitt's and leave it on her porch.

VIOLET. I wanna come.

IVAH. You can't.

VIOLET. But, I want to. *[Whining.]* I never get to do nothin'.

IVAH. 'Anything.' 'Nothin' is bad grammar. We used your hair ribbons, didn't we? Besides, I'm saving the very best for you, Vi.

VIOLET. *[Suspicious.]* What?

IVAH. After we do the breakfast dishes you and I will go over to ole lady Pruitt's and hid in the bushes and watch until she finds the perfume bottle.

VIOLET. We will?

IVAH. Yep. Now, come on....and not a word to Lillas or LaVerne.

VIOLET. Cross my heart *[SHE does the motions.]* and hope to die, stick a needle in my eye.

[*THEY exit. Then re-enter. They are sneaking through the bushes outside the Pruitt home.*]

VIOLET. *[Whispering.]* Where's the perfume bottle? I can't see it. Oh, no, it's gone. She's already found it...

IVAH. *[Whispering.]* Shhh....she'll hear you, ninny hammer. It's there. See? Over by the flower pot?

VIOLET. Oh, yeah.

IVAH. Stay down and be quiet.

VIOLET. I am. *[Beat.]* How long do you think we have to wait?

IVAH. *[Gleefully.]* As long as it takes.

*[Several beats. Suddenly the front door opens on the Pruitt house and a middle-aged woman comes out onto the porch. **HER** hair is up in rollers and she wears an old, torn bathrobe. She has old slippers on. **SHE** takes a deep breath of morning air.]*

WIDOW PRUITT. Ahhh!

*[Stretching and looking out at the beautiful morning. **SHE** scratches her arm pit. **SHE** picks up her broom and lazily sweeps the porch. **SHE** finally sees the pretty perfume bottle.]*

WIDOW PRUITT. Oh my, what do we have here?

*[**IVAH** and **VIOLET** poke each other and giggle. **MRS. PRUITT** picks the bottle and envelope up.]*

WIDOW PRUITT. Isn't this lovely? Oh, and a note...

*[**SHE** holds the bottle in her arm as **SHE** tears open the envelope and reads.]*

'From a secret admirer'....Oh my...

*[**SHE** fans herself with the envelope and then reads on.]*

...who worships you from afar'. Oh my!

*[Blushing, **SHE** looks around to see if anyone is witness to this declaration of love. **SHE** tucks the love letter and envelope in her robe next to her heart. **SHE**, with some difficulty, uncorks the bottle. **SHE** takes a deep inhale of the 'perfume', chokes, gasps and faints from the fumes. **IVAH** and **VIOLET** begin to giggle and then to laugh hysterically.]*

VIOLET. Shhh...shh. She's....gonna....hear us.
IVAH. *[Laughing hysterically.]* Ole lady Pruitt can't hear a thing....oh, no, I'm gonna pee my pants....Oh, Oh, that's the funniest thing I ever did see...
VIOLET. *[Sobering for a moment.]* You don't think she's dead, do you Ivy? Your farts are really stinky.
IVAH. No, she just fainted. She swooned over her secret lover.
VIOLET. She looks dead to me...
IVAH. *[Laughing.]* You are too serious for nine years old, ya know that, Vi? If you're so worried about her, go poke her to see if she's breathing.

VIOLET. Uh-uh. I'm not going up there.

IVAH. That's what I thought.   Come on, let's get outta here before she wakes up.

IVAH. You know what the worst part is, Vi?

VIOLET. No, what?

IVAH. We can't tell anybody....how are we gonna keep *this* a secret?

*[***THEY*** exit.]*

CURTAIN

IVAH THE TERRIBLE

by

Trisha Sugarek

CAST OF CHARACTERS

Arthur - He is a successful attorney.

Ivah - Ivah is NOT your typical housewife.

Mr. Hudson - The important client from Chicago.

Jimmy, Paperboy - Young boy.

Scene 1

Setting. The living room of an upscale home. A   door leads to the kitchen. Dinner hour.

> [**ARTHUR** *enters the front door. HE carries a briefcase.* **IVAH** *enters from the kitchen.*
> **IVAH** *is in shorts, dirt stains on her legs from working in the garden.*]

ARTHUR. Hi, Doll. I'm home from the salt mines, finally.
IVAH. Hi honey. *[She crosses to him and kisses him.]* How was court today? Did Judge Ratchet give you the contingency you needed?
ARTHUR. *[Embraces her.]* Yes, thank God. He's a good old bird underneath all that rough talk. Lord, Ivah, what are you wearing? Eu' de' Manure? I love you, but you stink! Digging in the garden today?
IVAH. Yep! *[Crossing to a drinks cart. Pours Arthur a sherry.]* And that's where you and I disagree, my love. I adore the smell of freshly turned earth. Then add a little manure for spice....Umm....

> [**SHE** *hands* **HIM** *the drink.* **ARTHUR** *crosses to* **HIS** *chair and sits.*]

ARTHUR. You can take the girl out of the country but you can't take the manure off of the girl. *[Beat.]* And I wouldn't change you for the world.
IVAH. *[Laughing.]* That's 'backwoods' to you, mister. I'm no farmer's daughter, even though you like to think so...I'm a woodsmen's daughter through and through and proud of it!
ARTHUR. Oh, please, allow me my dreams. I've always wanted to flirt with a farmer's daughter and right now you smell... *[Laughs.]* ..exactly how I would imagine she would smell.   Better go get cleaned up. I have an important client dropping in to sign some papers.
IVAH. Oh, Arty. I've got dinner on. Can't he come by the office tomorrow?

ARTHUR. No can do, sweetheart. He's on his way to the airport to catch the red eye back to Chicago. This is our only time to wind this up. Sorry. He won't stay long.

IVAH. In that case, I'm going to hide in the kitchen until he's gone. I don't have time to clean up before dinner. We'll eat in the kitchen tonight. *[Turns back.]* Chicago? Is this the guy who's so secretive? The one that's loaded with money?

ARTHUR. You have such a turn of phrase. Yes, he's the one...from Chicago...likes his privacy and if having millions is being 'loaded' then yes, it's the client you're thinking of.

IVAH. Oh, darn...I've always wanted to meet a real live multi-millionaire. Especially this one! He's so mysterious....I'm dying to see him

ARTHUR. *[Laughs.]* Well, you can't...looking and *smelling* like that.

IVAH. Another time, then.

> *[SHE pours HERSELF a sherry, crosses to the kitchen door.]*

I'll take myself and my sherry out to the kitchen and wait for you there. Hurry it up so dinner isn't ruined.

ARTHUR. He should be here any minute. I have the papers all ready for his signature. Ten minutes tops, love.

IVAH. See you in a bit, darling.

> *[SHE exits. ARTHUR lays the documents on the coffee table, sorting them briefly. The doorbell rings. ARTHUR rises, crosses to the door and opens it.]*

ARTHUR. Mr. Hudson, sir. Please come in.

> *[MR. HUDSON enters, wearing a dark suit and red tie. HE carries a briefcase.]*

MR. HUDSON. Arthur. Thank you for letting me stop by.

ARTHUR. It's my pleasure, sir. Won't you be seated?

> *[THEY cross to the living room.]*

The sofa there is quite comfortable.

MR. HUDSON. Just for a moment. *[Sits. Looking around the room.]* Very nice home you have, Arthur.

ARTHUR. Thank you. May I offer you a drink, sir? Perhaps a sherry?

MR. HUDSON. A small one perhaps.

> *[ARTHUR crosses to the drinks tray and pours a glass. HE crosses back to Mr. Hudson.]*

ARTHUR. This is from Portugal. Quite a decent vintage.

MR. HUDSON. Thank you. I don't have much time. My flight's at eight. I have my driver waiting.

[**ARTHUR** *sits.*]

ARTHUR. Yes, sir. Here are the papers you asked me to prepare. *[Turning them toward Mr. Hudson.]* I believe you will find everything in order.
MR. HUDSON. Excellent. I don't have time to read them in detail. I trust you have followed my instructions to the letter, Arthur?
ARTHUR. Precision Tool and Dye will be acquired on the first of the month, for a purchase price of one point eight million, payable over the next two years. The purchaser's name will be the corporate name and nowhere on the documents does your name appear. Upper management has agreed to stay on for at least the next twelve months. If you will sign here.... *[Turning the pages.]* and here.....and here....

[*As* **ARTHUR** *is shuffling the papers, there is a soft, tentative knock at the front door.* **ARTHUR** *rises.*]

ARTHUR. Who in the world? Excuse me, Sir. *[Crosses to the door and opens it.]* Oh! Hello, there, Jimmy.

[*The paperboy,* **JIMMY,** *hands* **ARTHUR** *the evening paper.*]

Thank you.

[*The* **BOY** *stands there waiting.*]

What can I do for you?
JIMMY. Collecting for the newspaper delivery, Mr. Gibbons.
ARTHUR. Can you come back tomorrow, Jimmy? I'm a little busy at the moment.
JIMMY. Gee, Mr. Gibbons...I'm late turning in my money. I have to get it all in by tomorrow. If you could....
ARTHUR. Oh, all right. How much is it, son?
JIMMY. Three bucks....er...dollars, Sir.

[**ARTHUR** *takes* **HIS** *wallet out and gives* **JIMMY** *a five dollar bill.*]

ARTHUR. Keep the change, Jimmy.
JIMMY. *[Looking at the two dollar tip.]* Golly, Geez, Mr. Gibbons...
ARTHUR. I appreciate good work, son.
JIMMY. Thanks a lot. Bye...
ARTHUR. You're welcome.

[ARTHUR closes the door with a firm slam and crosses back. HE sits.]

I am so sorry, Mr. Hudson.

MR. HUDSON. I heard. These youngsters today...always leaving everything to the last minute. Reminds me of my grandson.   I believe I've signed everything.   Best if you go through and double check....make certain you have what you need. I am most eager to complete this purchase.

ARTHUR. Yes, sir, of course.

[ARTHUR takes the documents and begins to go through them. HIS head is down. MR. HUDSON sits back, and glances around. The kitchen door silently swings open to reveal IVAH on her hands and knees, crawling through the doorway. SHE is still in her gardening shorts, HER hair is askew and there are smudges of dirt on her legs   and arms. As MR. HUDSON watches, IVAH crawls across the dining room floor, with great stealth. SHE crawls to the large bay window and, still on her knees, SHE cautiously parts the sheers and peeps out to get a look at the mysterious client who SHE thinks has just left. ARTHUR's attention is focused on the papers. HE has not seen Ivah.]

ARTHUR. These look fine, Mr. Hudson.   I will record them tomorrow and wire the first installment....

[MR. HUDSON bursts out laughing. ARTHUR looks stunned. At ARTHUR's voice and the sound of laughter, IVAH whirls around, aghast when SHE sees Mr. Hudson still seated in the living room. MR. HUDSON laughs harder. IVAH starts to grin. ARTHUR turns and sees IVAH, for the first time, kneeling by the window.]

ARTHUR. Ivah! My God, what are you doing?

[MR. HUDSON continues to chuckle. IVAH brazenly grins at Mr. Hudson.]

IVAH. Trying to get a good look at....well...at you! Hi, I'm Ivah, Arthur's wife. Would you like to stay for dinner?

CURTAIN

No Means NO!

by

Trisha Sugarek

CAST OF CHARACTERS

Emilee. Age 13, a pubescent girl making decisions

Danny.   Age 14, Emilee's first boyfriend

Maribeth. Age 22, Emilee's older sister

Emilee's best friends

Ruth. Age 13. The timid one
Barb. Age 14. The bold one
Sue. . Age 14.   The worrier

Note: Some sexual references.

Scene 1

Setting: A neighborhood park near a middle-school. Mid-afternoon.

(**EMILEE** *and* **DANNY** *are seated on a bench.* **THEY** *are sitting upstage with their backs to audience and are kissing.* **DANNY** *begins to fondle* **EMILEE**. **SHE** *pushes* **HIS** *hands away.)*

EMILEE. No! Cut it out Danny!
DANNY. *(Stopping.)* I want you, Emilee. Stop being such a tease.
EMILEE. *(Holding both of his wrists.)* I don't want to.

*(***DANNY*** begins to kiss her again.* **HE** *starts to touch her again. Jumping up,* **SHE** *yells at* **HIM**.*)*

EMILEE. I said 'No'! I don't want you to do that!
DANNY. I thought you loved me?
EMILEE. I do.
DANNY. Okay then.

*(***DANNY*** pulls* **HER** *down on to the bench.* **HE** *begins to kiss and fondle* **EMILEE** *again.)*

EMILEE. *(Jumping up and crossing several steps away.)* Stop it, Danny!

  (SHE *rushes off and exits.)*

DANNY. *(Rising and calling after her.)* Em! I love you!

Scene   2

Setting. Emilee's home.

(**SUE, RUTH** *and* **BARB** *are laughing and talking.* **EMILEE** *is not participating.*)

SUE. *(Noticing her friend.)* What's wrong, Em? You sick?
EMILEE. No. Nothing.
BARB. Come on, 'fess up. We've known you since first grade. What's the matter?
RUTH. You can tell us. You know that, right?
EMILEE. *(Sighing.)* It's Danny.
RUTH. Ugh! Boys!

(**THEY** *laugh except* **EMILEE.**)

SUE. Whad' he do?
BARB. Yeah, what? We'll beat him up for you.
EMILEE. *(Laughing tearfully.)* He…he wants to do stuff.
SUE. They all do.
BARB. Comes with dating, Em. They're all dogs.
RUTH. Yeah.
EMILEE. But, I don't wanna.

SUE. What?

EMILEE. You know…stuff. *(Beat.)* And I'm afraid that if I don't, he'll break up with me.

SUE. Yeah, there's that.

BARB. Just do it. It's not so bad if you close your eyes.

*(The **GIRLS** who are sexually active giggle.)*

RUTH. Do what?

SUE. Jimmy wanted me to kiss him…down there.

RUTH. Why?

EMILEE. I'm not doing that!

BARB. *(Blurts out.)* I'm having sex with Arnie.

*(The **GIRLS** scream.)*

SUE. No, you're not!

BARB. Am too.

RUTH. Barbara J. Masters! I'm telling your Mom!

BARB. No you're not, Ruthie. Remember our pledge.

SUE. I'm not having sex until I'm sixteen, at least. My parents promised me a car if I will abstain…their word…until I'm sixteen.

BARB. Car trumps a boyfriend any day.

SUE. But that doesn't mean we don't do other stuff.

RUTH. Barbie, you're using a condom, right?

BARB. Arnie doesn't like them.

RUTH. But you have to.

EMILEE. I don't want to do any of it. And Danny keeps after me every time we're alone. What should I do?

RUTH. You shouldn't do anything you don't want to, Em.

BARB. Like I said, it's not so bad. And if you don't, Danny will find someone who will give him what he wants. He's so cute!

SUE. I can't wait until I'm older. It's so hard being thirteen.

Scene   3

Setting. The park bench.

>(**DANNY** and **EMILEE** sit downstage facing the audience. HIS arm is loosely draped over her shoulders. **HE** holds **HER** hand.)

DANNY. Come on, Em. We're going steady and all the other kids are doin' it. Your friends do it.
EMILEE. But, Danny, I don't want to. And not all the other kids are having sex.
DANNY. All your friends are.

>(**EMILEE** snatches **HER** hand away and shrugs **DANNY'S** arm off her shoulders. **SHE** moves away from him on the bench.)

EMILEE. That's not true! Who told you that?
DANNY. The guys…Jimmy and Arnie and some of my other friends.
EMILEE. (Mumbles.) That's doesn't mean I have to.
DANNY. What?
EMILEE. (Louder.) I said that doesn't mean that I have to.
DANNY. (Staring at her. Beat.) Well, it does if you want to be my girlfriend.
EMILEE. (Shocked.) Danny!

DANNY. Look. I'm sorry but I'm a normal guy who needs things. All my friends are getting it. How does it make me look if I'm not?

EMILEE. Are you saying I'm not normal?

DANNY. *(Sighing.)* No.

EMILEE. Danny, I love you, but I'm just not ready.

DANNY. *(Standing.)* Okay. Let me know when you are.

EMILEE. Are you breaking up with me?

DANNY. Yeah, I guess I am.

(**DANNY** *exits.*)

Scene   4

Setting. Emilee's living room.

> *(**EMILEE** sits on the sofa in the dusk. **SHE** stars at nothing. **MARIBETH**, her older sister enters, and turns on a light.)*

MARIBETH. *(Startled.)* Emilee, you scared me out of a year of my life. Where's Mom?
EMILEE. *(Subdued.)* Sorry. *(Beat.)* She has to work late.

> *(**MARIBETH** flops down in a chair and kicks **HER** shoes off.)*

MARIBETH. Whew! What a day.

> *(**EMILEE** does not respond. Silence. A few beats.)*

MARIBETH. *(Parroting what her sister's response should have been.)* 'What happened at work? As your baby sister, I'm always interested in your day.'
EMILEE. Huh? Oh yeah. How was your day?
MARIBETH. I almost got fired. I had to use every last second of a deadline to deliver.
EMILEE. *(Not really listening.)* Uh-huh.
MARIBETH. And then this huge giraffe came waltzing in and knocked my desk over and peed on my computer.
EMILEE. *(Sits up.)* Wait! What?

MARIBETH. You're not even listening. I don't know why I bother.

EMILEE. Sorry. *(Beat.)* Why are you home in the middle of the week?

MARIBETH. You mean besides Wednesday being hamburger night in Mom's kitchen? They're spraying my apartment for bugs and we all had to get out for twenty-four hours.

EMILEE. Oh.

MARIBETH. What's wrong with you, Em?

EMILEE. Danny.

MARIBETH. Oh. Trouble in paradise?

EMILEE. Why can't guys be more like the heroes in the romances we love to read? Danny's never romantic.

MARIBETH. Welcome to the real world. Wha'd Danny do besides being a guy?

EMILEE. I can't tell you…it's too embarrassing.

MARIBETH. Em, it's your big sister sitting here. Who else you gonna tell? *(Sighing.)* Come on, what did Danny do?

EMILEE. He broke up with meee!

MARIBETH. Oh, oh. Why?

EMILEE. *(Buries her face in her hands and mumbles.)* I don't want to do what he wants.

MARIBETH. Honey, I can't hear you.

EMILEE. *(Raises her head; almost yelling.)* He wants to do sex things!

MARIBETH. *(Trying not to smile.)* Oh.

EMILEE. I don't want to, Mar'!

MARIBETH. What do your friends say?

EMILEE. Some of them have actually had sex with their boyfriends and almost all of them do what the guy asks for so they can keep dating them.

MARIBETH. All of them?

EMILEE. I don't think Ruthie has. But who can tell? She doesn't even have a boyfriend right now. She's pretty quiet on the subject when we get together.

MARIBETH. Do you want my opinion?

EMILEE. *(Looks down, groaning.)* I don't think I can talk about this with my sister.

MARIBETH. Who better? It was just a few years ago that I was going through the same thing.

EMILEE. You were? But, you were so cool and popular when you were thirteen. I was just a little kid but I could see that your friends looked up to you.

MARIBETH. *(Smiled.)* That's because I knew I had options.

EMILEE. How? How did you know that?

MARIBETH. Mom told me. So I'm going to tell you what our Mom told me.

(EMILEE is silent but is listening.)

MARIBETH. Do you know your options? Do you know that you don't have to do anything you don't want to do?

EMILEE. *(Embarrassed.)* I'm having a bad dream…

MARIBETH. Being embarrassed and finding it hard to talk about is a sure sign that you're feeling pressured. Never let a boy pressure you.

EMILEE. *(Hides her face again.)* O.M.G.

MARIBETH. Listen, I'm just going to come right out and ask you. Are you sexually active at all?

EMILEE. Let me repeat. O.M.G.

MARIBETH. It's a yes or no answer, Em.

EMILEE. *(Sighing.)* No.

MARIBETH. Okay then. Do you have any questions at this time?

EMILEE. I'm mixed up. Some of my friends are doing other stuff besides having sex. Is that okay?

MARIBETH. Like…?

EMILEE. *(Groaning.)* I can't say it out loud to my sister. O.M.G.

MARIBETH. It's okay, I get the idea. All of it is 'having sex' in some fashion or another. And if you're not ready *(Beat.)* which I sincerely hope you are not…you have options. It is your decision, not some boy who wants your body.

EMILEE. Can we please stop talking about this? Pleeesse?

MARIBETH. Sure. Promise me one thing.

EMILEE. What?

MARIBETH. Promise to tell me before you do anything so we can discuss your options.

EMILEE. I promise. *(Beat.)* But what do I do about Danny?

MARIBETH. If he doesn't respect you enough to respect your decision then he's not worth your time.

EMILEE. Yeah, I guess.

(THEY are both silent.)

MARIBETH. *(Rising.)* Let's surprise Mom and get all the fixin's prepped for the hamburgers, whad'ya say?

EMILEE. *(Rising.)* Okay. *(Beat.)* You won't tell Mom will you?

MARIBETH. Of course not.

(SHE slings her arm around EMILEE.)

Come on, little sis, let's get cookin'.

(Exit.)

Scene   5

Setting. The night of prom. Emilee's house.

(**EMILEE** *and* **RUTH** *sit in the living room, in* **THEIR** *pj's watching a movie.*)

RUTH. *(Sighing.)* Who needs to go to a dumb old prom anyway? Who needs boys?
EMILEE. *(Sighing.)* Yeah, right? I just wish we could have been with Barb and Sue tonight.
RUTH. I'll bet they're having a good time without us.
EMILEE. I know, right?
RUTH. I didn't want to say in front of the others, Em, but when I started dating Chris…you remember him…I had the same problems as you did with Danny. He was always after me to go further than kissing.
EMILEE. Really. Why didn't tell us? I thought I was the weird geek who wouldn't do what everybody else was doing.
RUTH. I was too embarrassed. The one boyfriend I had and I ruined it.
EMILEE. I don't think we are the ones that have ruined anything. I think these boys ruined it for us!
RUTH. I guess.
EMILEE. My sister helped me see that if I'm not ready, I'M. NOT. READY. And that's okay. Think how bad we'd feel after if we let some boy pressure us into something we don't want to do.
RUTH. *(Sitting up straight.)* You know? Your sister's really smart. 'No' means no!
EMILEE. I'm not sure how good Barb and Susie feel about themselves.
RUTH. What do you mean? They're so popular.
EMILEE. Remember? The other day Barb said, 'if you close your eyes, it's not so bad'. That seems wrong somehow.

(A knock, OFF. **EMILEE** *rises and crosses OFF.* **SHE** *screams.* **BARB** *and* **SUE** *enter with their sleeping bags followed by* **EMILEE.** **RUTH** *squeals and rises. Crossing,* **RUTH** *hugs* **BARB** *and* **SUE.** **THEY** *all speak simultaneously.)*

RUTH. What are you doing here?

EMILEE. Oh guys! I'm so happy you're here.

BARB. Where else would we be?

SUE. We came to sleep over too.

*(***THEY*** cross into the living room and settle in chairs.* **BARB** *and* **SUE** *throw their bags on the floor.)*

RUTH. But you're missing prom!

BARB. *(Smirks.)* What prom?

SUE. Yeah, there's no prom if the four of us can't go together.

BARB. *(Grabbing a bowl.)* Yum! Popcorn!

EMILEE. But what did Arnie and Jimmy say?

*(***SUE*** and* **BARB** *exchange looks.)*

BARB. *(Shrugging.)* They're taking other girls.

RUTH. Oooo! Who?

SUE. Brittany and Alissa.

EMILEE. But…they're *(Beat.)*

BARB. Sluts?

RUTH. Barb!

SUE. It's true. They don't have the best reputations.

BARB. I told Arnie no way was he going without me. That was a deal breaker.

RUTH. What did he say?

BARB. He said he wasn't missing prom for anybody. So I guess we broke up.

EMILEE. What about Jimmy, Sue?

SUE. You know Jimmy. Where Arnie leads, Jimmy is trailing right behind him. I told him he couldn't go. *(Grimace.)* You see how that worked out.

RUTH. Are you breaking up with them?

BARB. Duh!

SUE. Of course. *(Beat.)*

BARB. *(Avoiding anyone's eyes.)* My period's five days late.

RUTH. Barbie!

SUE. That's a maj problem.

EMILEE. What're you going to do?

BARB. Wait. *(Beat.)* My mom's gonna kill me!

RUTH. But you told us your mom put you on birth control pills.

BARB. I might have missed one or two.

EMILEE. Oh, Barb, I'm sorry.

RUTH. Barb! How could you?

BARB. I'm done having sex. It's not worth it. If my period doesn't show up there goes college and everything.

RUTH. I heard hot baths helps.

EMILEE. That's just an old wives tale. Medical research says none of that stuff works. The only way to not get pregnant, one hundred percent, is to not have sex.

SUE. Who says?

EMILEE. My sister, Maribeth.

RUTH. She is so fab!

BARB. Besides, I didn't really like it. Brittany's welcome to Arnie if she wants him!

EMILEE. I think we're all too young.

RUTH. I agree.

SUE. I think we should make a pact. None of us should have sex until further notice. If we stand together on this, the boys can't pressure us to do stuff.

BARB. I'm in. The idea of maybe being preggers has really scared me!

EMILEE. I agree. Danny or any other boy is not worth doing something we don't want to do.

SUE. So we're all agreed? What should we swear on? A blood oath?

RUTH. I think a pinky-swear is good enough, Susie. Blood does not need to be spilt.

CURTAIN

BLACK vs. WHITE vs. BROWN

by

Trisha Sugarek

CAST OF CHARACTERS

Nicolle ~~ a beautiful Latina girl from Honduras

Maria ~~ Nicolle's friend from Mexico

Lilian ~~ Nicolle's friend from Honduras

Brittany ~~ a blond, cheerleader-type girl running for Winter Royalty

Tyron ~~ an African-American senior running for King

Tanisha ~~ an African-American senior also running for Queen of Winter Royalty

James ~~ a junior running for King

Mr. Brown ~~ Drama teacher and Vice-Principal
Dr. Abrams ~~ Principal of school

The Greek Chorus:

Text #1
Text #2
Text #3
Text #4

Escort: Juan Flores (double cast)

Author's note: Some profanity. Can be replaced but keep in mind this is how our teens speak and text.

Teen Slang 2018

Since the short plays are produced all over the world, a glossary is provided here:

Bruh–A casual nickname for "bro"
Idts.--I don't think so
Ngl-- not gonna lie
Fam–Their closest friends
GOAT–Acronym for "Greatest of all time!"
TBH–Acronym for "To be honest"
It's lit–Short for "It's cool or awesome!"
I'm weak–Short for "That was funny!"
Hundo P–Short for 100% sure or certain
Gucci–Something is good or cool
Squad–Term for their friend group
Bae–Short for "baby." It's used as a term of endearment for a significant other such as a girlfriend or boyfriend. As an acronym, it stands for "Before Anyone Else."
Curve–To reject someone romantically
Low Key–A warning that what they're saying isn't something they want everyone to know
Salty–To be bitter about something or someone
Skurt–To go away or leave
Throw shade–To give someone a nasty look or say something unpleasant about them.
Straight fire–Something is hot or trendy
Sip tea–To mind your own business
Thirsty–Being desperate for something
Down in the DM–Short for plans in their social media or texts for an oncoming sexual hook-up
Smash–To have casual sex
Netflix 'n Chill–To meet under the pretense of watching Netflix/TV together when actually planning to meet for "making out" or sex
NIFOC–Acronym for "Naked in front of their computer"
CU46–Acronym for "See you for sex"
9–Short for "A parent is watching!"
GNOC–Acronym for "Get naked on camera!"

Same--when you agree with something; sometimes used sarcastically; an easy response to anything and everything.

Too real--too relatable, hitting too close to home.

LFG-- let's f*cking go.

NFW--no f*cking way.

Send it-- just do it!!

Sipping tea--throwing shade, talking trash.

Can't even--when something is too ridiculous or funny or strange.

Scene   1

Setting: The halls of a high school. A couple of posters are on the walls urging students to vote for Winter Royalty.

    *(**NICOLLE** is at her locker with two of her Hispanic friends. **TANISHA** and **TYRON** in another group. **BRITTANY** and **JAMES** are in a third group.)*

MARIA. *(Leaning against the lockers.)* I know you're going to win, Nicolle. You're sooo popular.
NICOLLE. We'll see. Tanisha's very popular too.
LILIAN. *(Sighing.)* She always wins. But you're much prettier, Nic.
NICOLLE. I don't know about that but thanks Lilian.
TANISHA. *(Shooting a dirty look across the hallway.)* We should win, Tyron. We always win.
TYRON. *(Laughs.)* My Mama always tells me not to count my chickens before they hatch.
TANISHA. I don't even know what that means. I *do* know that you'll win. After all you're the president of our class, straight-A student and a member of the National Guard. You don't even hav'ta worry.
TYRON. We'll see.

    *(**TANISHA** stares at **TYRON**.)*

TYRON. *(Looks up from tapping on his phone.)* What?
TANISHA. Well, do you think I'm gonna win?
TYRON. Oh! For sure.
TANISHA. I just have to! I'm thirsty.

BRITTANY. Do you think Tanisha will win again this year?

JAMES. Hundo P— *(Beat.)* Maybe. I don't know.

BRITTANY. I'm happy to see you're so decisive, Jimmy.

JAMES. Don't call me that. You make me feel like we're back in fourth grade. It's James.

BRITTANY. *(Laughing.)* I'm weak.

JAMES. It's not funny, Brit.

(*The* **TEXTERS** *enter.* **THEY** *sit, lean, stand, concentrating on their mobile devices.* **THEY** *read aloud as they Snap-Chat.*)

Text #1. Who are you voting for?

Text #2. Duh…Tyron of course.

Text #3. I'm sure not voting for any Mexican!

Text #4. Tanisha! She's GOAT!

Text #2. I'd vote for her if she'd get NIFOC.

Text #3. Ugh.

Text #1. What about Brittany?

Text #2. She's stuck up.

Text #3. James is queer.

Text #4. Oh yeah.

Text #1. Brittany's okay.

Text #3. I'd smash me some of that.

Text #2. So is anyone voting for Nicolle?

Text #4. Did you see what she was wearing today-Gucci!

Text #3. She's still wet from swimmin' across the river.

Text #4. Ha. Ha.

Text #1. The Mexicans are taking over.

Text #2. I don't know, Fam, she's pretty enough she could win.

(*The* **TEXTERS** *exit, heads down, still tapping on their phones. The other* **STUDENTS** *put* **THEIR** *phones away.*)

BRITTANY. Do you know your lines?

JAMES. Of course. We're off book tonight. What about you Brit?

BRITTANY. I'm still shaky on Act two.

JAMES. You'll be fine once you get up on stage.

BRITTANY. The voting is Friday for Winter Royalty. Are you doing anything special to campaign?

JAMES. I asked each of my teachers, in each class, if I could say a few words before class starts.

BRITTANY. Ooo…good idea. How'd that go?

JAMES. Four out of the six teachers said 'yes'.

BRITTANY. What'd you say?

JAMES. You know. The usual. Listed my accomplishments, plug our new play opening, ask for their vote…blah, blah, blah.

BRITTANY. That's lit.

JAMES. I know, right?

BRITTANY. James, do me a huge fav. Snap Chat to our Squad a 'vote for Brittany'. Would you? I'm thirsty.

JAMES. Sure. I'll do it between my classes. Gotta skurt. See you at rehearsal after school.

BRITTANY. See ya.

   (JAMES exits. **NICOLLE** *catches up to* **HER** *friends.)*

MARIA. Are you finished campaigning, Nic?

NICOLLE. No, I've got one more idea.

LILIAN. What?

NICOLLE. Thursday, right before the election I'm going to hand out candy in my classes.

MARIA. That's Gucci!

LILIAN. Will the teachers let you?

NICOLLE. *(Laughing.)* If I offer them candy first.

   (A school bell sounds.)

MARIA. I have to hurry. My next class is clear across campus.

LILIAN. See you after school. Bye.

NICOLLE. See you later.

   (The **GIRLS** *hurry off in different directions.)*

TANISHA. You're so lucky, Ty.

TYRON. What? Why?

TANISHA. You're a guy.

TYRON. So?

TANISHA. All the girls in the school love you. Think you're Goat. And all the guys want to *be* you.

TYRON. Uh-uh. I'm just a regular guy.

TANISHA. Bruh…you're straight fire. Don't deny it.

TYRON. I think James has a real shot at it. Him having the lead in the school play. He's a good guy for being white and all.

TANISHA. Is that the best shade ya got, Ty?

TYRON. I'm just sayin'. *(Beat.)* Oh-oh, we're gonna be late.

TANISHA. I've got study hall.

TYRON. I gotta get goin'. I've got Chem.

     *(**THEY** wander stage left in no particular hurry.)*

TANISHA. You got practice after school?

TYRON. Every day.

TANISHA. Okay, then I guess I'll see you tomorrow.

Scene   2

Setting: High school. Day of the election.

(TEXTERS are on stage. THEY are upstage, staring at their mobile devices. TYRON is standing outside his first class-room, handing out small flyers. As HIS classmates pass by he hands them a flyer.)

TYRON. Hey, Brian. Vote for me, Bruh.
TYRON. *(To the next student.)* Would like to get your vote.
TYRON. Vote for Tyron Johnson.

(As the STUDENTS pass by, THEY smile, grunt, punch TYRON on the arm. TANISHA enters and crosses to TYRON.)

TANISHA. Hey, Ty.
TYRON. *(Continues to hand out flyers as he talks.)* Was'up, Tanisha?
TANISHA. Can I stand here with you?
TYRON. Not a problem. Why?
TANISHA. Well, we are the reigning King and Queen. It won't hurt to be seen together and —since you're handing out flyers anyways, it'll help me too.
TYRON. Sure. Fine with me. *(Hands a flyer to another classmate.)* Appreciate your vote.
TANISHA. *(As other classmates pass by.)* Vote for your reigning King and Queen.
TYRON. Are you worried about Nicolle running too?
TANISHA. *(Looks at him, shocked.)* TBH? *(Beat.)* Dhuh. No. She's Mexican. Doesn't stand a chance against me.
TYRON. She's popular around school. *(Continues to hand out flyers.)* Vote for Tyron Johnson.

TANISHA. *(Plastering a fake smile on.)* Vote for your King and Queen today. *(Out of the side of her mouth she murmurs.)* Ty, why are you talkin' that way? Whose side are you on?
TYRON. *(Beat.)* Yours, of course. I'm just sayin'.

*(***TYRON*** and ***TANISHA*** get alerts on ***THEIR*** phones and begin to read their mobile devices as…)*

Text #1. Big day today. Who's the Fam voting for?
Text #2. Tyron and Tanisha all the way.
Text #3. I don't know. TBH, Nicolle's awfully cute.
Text #4. Do you think she'd smash for a vote?
Text #1. Idts. You douche.
Text #2. Who's voting for Tanisha?
Text #3. Ngl. She's gotten a little stuck up, winning every year.
Text #4. Same.
Text #2. U r sipping tea.
Text #1. Too real. I'm voting for James and Nicolle.
Text #2. No way!
Text #3. Im shook. You gotta vote to Ty and Tanish.
Text #4. LFG. Voting ends in two hours.
Text #2. So Tyron is our King, so who's our Queen?
Send it. Vote for Tanisha!
Text #3. Nope. Not this year.
Text #4. Can't even. I'm voting for Nicolle.
Text #1. But she's Mexican!
Text #3. Yeah, nobody's voting for the little brown girl.
Text #4. I am.
Text #1. Another year of jungle monkey royal court? NFW. Vote Brittany and James!

Scene   3

Setting. Drama Class.

> *(**MR. BROWN** sits in a chair watching **HIS** students file in. **NICOLLE** crosses to **HIM**. **SHE** holds a garbage bag.)*

NICOLLE. Mr. Brown, can I pass out candy before class starts?

> *(**SHE** holds open the bag and offers **MR. BROWN** candy. **HE** reaches in and takes a couple of pieces.)*

MR. BROWN. Thanks. What's it for?
NICOLLE. *(Grins.)* Trying to get votes.
MR. BROWN. Ah. Sweetening up your constituents, huh?
NICOLLE. Yeah. Is it okay?
MR. BROWN. Sure. If I can have another Tootsie-Roll.
NICOLLE. *(Offers him the bag again.)* Sure.
MR. BROWN. Thanks.

> *(**NICOLLE** turns to **HER** classmates and offers the bag of candy.)*

MARIA. Candy!
LILIAN. Gucci!

> *(**BRITTANY** and **JAMES** gather around and help **THEMSELVES** to candy too.)*

BRITTANY. Great idea, Nicolle.
NICOLLE. Thanks, Brit. Good luck today.
BRITTANY. Same to you, Nic. I think you're gonna win.
JAMES. Shhh. Don't jinx it by using the 'W' word.
NICOLLE. *(Laughing.)* James, I think you have a good chance of WU'ing.
JAMES. *(Sticking his fingers in his ears.)* La, la, la, la, la.
MARIA. This is so Gucci. Love the Reese's cups.

*(The **GROUP** of friends all laugh.)*

MR. BROWN. Okay, class. Find your seats, please. Candy time is over. Before we start talking about fleshing out your characters, I want to mention the elections for Winter Royalty. I'm very proud of you who are running for King and Queen. I couldn't help but overhear your conversation. As candidates, Brittany, Nicolle, and James, you are acting with integrity, fairness and positivity. Supporting your fellow candidates is very mature.

*(The **STUDENTS** playfully boo **MR. BROWN**.)*

NICOLLE. *(Laughing.)* Boo—boo.
MARIA. Boo.
LILIAN. Boo.
BRITTANY. Boo.
JAMES. *(Singing.)* Boo-de-boo-dee-boo, boo, boo.
MR. BROWN. Okay you comedians, settle down. Homework was developing rich characters from your assigned parts. I asked that you describe their bedrooms, in detail. Who wants to go first?

(Hands shoot up.)

Scene 4

Setting. After-school assembly. King and Queen of Winter Royalty to be announced.

(The principal, **DR. ABRAMS** *and vice-principal,* **MR. BROWN** *are in the middle of   the room, holding microphones. The* **TEXTERS** *are on stage mingled in with everyone.)*

DR. ABRAMS. Okay, people, settle down. We are here to announce the new King and Queen for Winter Royalty and the prom. Every year we run several campaigns and elections; one being for the Royalty. Hopefully this gives the student-body a taste of politics and more importantly, voting when you reach age eighteen. Now I'll hand it over to your drama coach and campaign advisor, Mr. Brown.

*(***ALL** *the students yell and clap and stomp their feet [on the bleachers];* **MR. BROWN** *is very popular.)*

MR. BROWN. *(Making a theatrical bow.)* Thank you, thank you, thank you. Now sit down so that we can find out who are the new King and Queen.

(Stragglers of clapping and hooting are heard.)

First, let us introduce the reigning King and Queen, Tyron Johnson and Tanisha Brocton.

*(***TYSON,** *with* **TANISHA** *on his arm, enter.* **THEY** *cross to center and stand a little left of the two teachers.)*

I would like to now introduce the candidates for this year. Of course, as is our tradition, our reigning King and Queen are also candidates.

*(As **MR. BROWN** announces their names the **STUDENTS** enter as couples, taking **THEIR** place on the other side of Mr. Brown.)*

Nicolle Escobar on the arm of escort, Juan Flores. Brittany Andersen and James Abbott.

*(**STUDENTS** clap and hoot for their favorites.)*

MR. BROWN. Without further to do, the envelopes, please, Dr. Abrams.

*(**DR. ABRAMS** hands **MR. BROWN** two white envelopes.)*

MR. BROWN. Thank you.

*(**HE** looks up and grins at the audience.)*

Are you ready for the results?

(More clapping and yelling.)

NICOLLE. *(Murmuring to no one in particular.)* The suspense is killing me.
BRITTANY. *(Whispering.)* Now we know why he's the drama teacher.
JAMES. *(Giggling.)* He really knows how to work a crowd.
TYRON. Come on, Mr. Brown. You're makin' me sweat!
MR. BROWN. Okay, okay.

*(**HE** rips open the first envelope.)*

MR. BROWN. The new King for Winter Royalty is…Tyron Johnson!

*(**STUDENTS** yell and clap.)*

TANISHA. *(Smiling up at Tyron, she whispers.)* We won again, Ty.
TYRON. *(Smiling.)* Looks like it, Tanisha.

*(**TYRON** crosses to **MR. BROWN** who shakes **HIS** hand as the assembly claps and hollers.)*

MR. BROWN. Congratulations, Tyron.

TYRON. Thank you, Mr. Brown.

*(**TYRON** looks at the audience and waves. **HE** leans over to the microphone that **MR. BROWN** holds.)*

TYRON. Thanks for your support everyone.
MR. BROWN. And now for the new Queen— *(Ripping open the other envelope.)* Our new Queen is…

*(So certain that **SHE** has won, **TANISHA** takes a step forward.)*

MR. BROWN. Ta…*(He stumbles as he starts to read the wrong name. Recovers quickly.)* NICOLLE ESCOBAR!

*(**MARIA, LILIAN** and **BRITTANY** all run to **NICOLLE**, who is laughing and crying. **JAMES** hugs **HER**.)*

JAMES. Congrats, doll! I knew you'd win!
NICOLLE. James, what just happened?
JAMES. You won, girlfriend! Can I be in your court?
MARIA. *(Hugging her friend.)* Nic, you're our Queen!
LILIAN. *(Jumping up and down.)* You won! You won!
BRITTANY. Congratulations, Nic. You deserve it.
NICOLLE. *(Hugs Brittany.)* Thanks, Brit. Will you be part of my court?
BRITTANY. Really?

*(The minute the results are announced, the **TEXTERS** begin tapping on their devices, slowly crossing to stage left until **THEY** are a group separate from the others. **THEY** continue to Snap-Chat frantically.)*

Text #1. What? What just happened?
Text #2. I can't believe this.
Text #3. Idts.
Text #4. Tanisha lost?
Text #1. WTF?
Text #2. I'm so salty!
Text #3. No way!

(**TANISHA** *reluctantly crosses to* **NICOLLE. DR. ABRAMS** *removed the crown from* **TANISHA**'s *head and places it on* **NICOLLE**'s. **TANISHA** *smiles sickly at the new Queen and moves off.* **TYRON** *takes* **HIS** *place next to* **NICOLLE.** *The* **STUDENTS** *cheer.*)

TYRON. Congrats, girl.
NICOLLE. Thanks, Ty.
TYRON. You ran a great campaign.
NICOLLE. Thanks. You're not mad because Tanisha didn't win, are you?
TYRON. Naw. Keepin' it low key but I'm happy for you. The school needs some shakin' up.
NICOLLE. It's so Lit—I never thought I'd win against Tanisha. She's so Gucci.
TYRON. She is.
NICOLLE. What do we do next?
TYRON. Be queenly! *(Laughing. Beat.)* Ya wanna go to prom with me?

(**ALL** *exit except for the* **TEXTERS** *who are frantically Snap-Chatting.* **EVERYONE**'s *phones chirp, ding and blow up with texts coming in.*)

Text #3. A Mexican won?
Text #4. NFW!
Text #1. That little wet-back is our Queen?
Text #1. At least the fag didn't win.
Text #2. I'm totally salty!
Text #3. It was rigged!
Text #2. They messed with the ballots.
Text #4. The Mexicans rigged it for sure.
Text #3. Can't even.
Text #2. I hate Mexicans. They're dirty and lazy.
Text #4. We should protest. A sit-in. Stay woke!
Text #2. F**king Mexicans.
Text #1. My Dad says they're all illegal.
Text #2. Too real.
Text #3. I can't even.
Text #4. At least Ty is our King…but the brown girl is Queen?
Text #1. The Squad should black-ball the prom.
Text #2. NFW. I'm not missin' prom.
Text #1. We have to go to support Tyron.
Text #4. How did this happen?
Text #3. Ngl. I thought Tanisha would win. *I* voted for her, did you?

(Silence. The texting dies. The **TEXTERS** *stay on stage looking down at their devices. Beat.)*

CURTAIN

Turn the Page for a Bonus Play!

POSSESSION IS NINE TENTHS

by

Trisha Sugarek

Full length, two Acts, 60 minutes

NOTICE

Artwork by Lori Smaltz

CAST OF CHARACTERS

The band of Spirits:

Chance ....The organizer. Male   [double cast/Rev. Tuttle].

Vague ....The peacemaker and gentle spirit played by a female

 [double cast/Mrs. Tuttle].

Baubles..... played by an extravagantly dressed male. He is never still, either posing, prancing, or dancing.

Chaos.......The trouble maker who claims she is mathematically perfect.
                    Played by a female.

The Family:

Kate..... Ben and Claire's mother, she is in her late thirties.

Rory .....Their father, he is in his early forties.

Claire....Kate and Rory's daughter, twelve years old,
suffering from leukemia.

Ben.......Kate and Rory's son, a bright precocious eight years old.

Reverend Tuttle...A pompous blowhard.

Mrs. Tuttle...The Reverend's wife, mousy and quiet.

4 m.
4 f.

Production Notes

The abandoned lighthouse should be created by lighting and fog to create the illusion of dirt and debris. The second Scene opens with the moving company arriving and moving the Fullers furnishings in. The audience watches this Scene change.

The incorrect references to computer hardware is on purpose and not typos.

As the story proceeds, the spirits, Chance and Vague leave and the parts of Chance/Tuttle and Vague/Mrs. Tuttle are double cast.

Chaos and Baubles become Ben's imaginary friends and are frequently on stage talking and playing with Ben and Claire, while the adults interact as if they aren't there. The adults cannot see or hear the spirits. Ben's names for Chaos and Baubles are Charlie and Henry.

The moving men are stage crew in overalls. They should enter with furniture and boxes. Except for a box of linens and books, most of the boxes are carried on and immediately off into other 'rooms'.

Baubles should have as many costume changes as the budget allows; each one more outrageous than the last.

Page 20 if the actor cast as Ben hasn't lost any teeth, a tooth can be blacked out or referred to in the back of the mouth, by Mrs. Tuttle.

Hair color may be changed on page 50 according to the actor that is cast.

For Baubles and Chaos' final exit, they should appear to pass through a solid wall.

Songs: Purple People Eater, Cabaret, and Somewhere Over the Rainbow and The Rain in Spain. Rights must be obtained from ASCAP and credit must be given in the program.

Place
Interior of an old, deserted lighthouse

Time
Present

This play is based upon a true story, told here, about the men of the Coast Guard manning a lighthouse and saving the life of a fisherman with the help of a spirit.

ACT I
Scene   1

Setting. An empty abandoned space. Pale blue light streams in through the dirty windows.
A discarded cardboard box and a broken chair litter the floor. A rickety wooden ladder
stands by the upstage wall and windows.

*[CHANCE enters with broom and cleaning materials. VAGUE wanders the stage.
THEY are dressed in robes with hoods.]*

CHANCE. *[Frantically begins to clean and sweep.]* Really, Vague, we must clean this place up.
What will they think?
VAGUE. *[In a vague voice.]* Yes...we will, Chance. How does tomorrow sound?
CHANCE. Everything is tomorrow with you. Have you forgotten that they will be here tomorrow?
Where's your gumption? Chaos and Baubles will be here any minute and we must all pitch in and
get the job done.

[VAGUE has floated up the ladder and is watching out the window.]

VAGUE. Do you think that if I watch from here, I will see them coming?
CHANCE. Vague!   Have you been listening to a thing I have said. They will arrive tomorrow and
we must make a good impression.   What if they change their minds, what if they don't want to
occupy?
VAGUE. Do you think that's a possibility? Oh, my.
CHANCE. Oh, my, indeed. Well? Are you going to help or not?
VAGUE. Yes, I suppose I can do a little.

[In a quick blackout VAGUE disappears. Suddenly dust and motes rain down on CHANCE.]

CHANCE. *[Looks up.]* What in heaven or hell are you doing up there? Cut it out! I'm   getting dirt all over me....
VAGUE. *[Off. With a series of sneezes.]*
Chance! Language!
 CHANCE. Sorry.
VAGUE. I'm cleaning out the cobwebs. I said I'd help.

[With more sneezes, additional dust and debris falls from the ceiling.]

CHANCE. Vague, float on down here immediately!   You're making everything worse.

[From the black curtain, upstage, VAGUE's face appears.]

VAGUE. Here I am.   What's the matter? *[Sees CHANCE covered in dirt.]* Oh, dear.
CHANCE. 'Oh dear', indeed. Never mind. I'll do it myself. Go and be our lookout until the others get here. Then we'll all pitch in and clean up this place.

[Suddenly there is 'Lisa Minnelli' music and BAUBLES enters. Prancing on, HE is dressed in the same robes as the other spirits, but HIS robes are in fluorescent tie-die colors. HIS hair is green and HIS high heeled pumps are covered in red sequins. BAUBLES strikes a pose.]

BAUBLES. *[Speaking in the third person.]* We're here.....my pets. Lisa incarnate! How do you like our hair? We just had it done.
VAGUE. *[Vague, HE considers his hair style.]* I think I like it, Baubles.
CHANCE. So, that's the way you plan to appear when our new tenants arrive? Don't you think it's a trifle loud?   I can hardly hear myself think looking at you.
BAUBLES. Darling...is hims just a trifle jealous?   I'm one of the few on the circuit who can pull this look off....I'm tall and slim so I can wear just about anything.
CHANCE. *[Dryly.]* Oh yes, that must be it....I'm jealous.
[CHAOS arrives twirling, jumping, throwing confetti and sparkles into the air. Cymbals crash, lots of noise.]
CHANCE. Good grief, Chaos! Pipe down. And stop making such a mess. I'm trying to clean up....
CHAOS. Chaos is perfect. Mathematically perfect. And I'm not making a mess. I am decorating the place for our new tenants. Our Coasties loved my chaotic ways. And they adored my pranks.

VAGUE. Oh....I miss them so much!   Why did they go away, Chance?

[*CHANCE ignores VAGUE.*]

CHANCE. The Coast Guard boys didn't know the difference between their dirty underwear and your 'decorating'.

CHAOS. But, they loved me.   And you too, Baubles.   Remember what fun we had gluing the toilet seats up, putting salt in the sugar bowl, short sheeting the beds, turning off the hot water....

BAUBLES. Oh yes!   Those dear boys.   What a party we had.   I miss them too.

CHAOS. Until that smelly, old fisherman had to spoil everything.

CHANCE. Our boys were never the same after seeing him, were they?

BAUBLES. That's all the excuse the Coast Guard needed to shut the lighthouse down and go automated.......what is automated?   Exactly?

VAGUE. It's gigi-a-bits, and SD Ram and DVD Rome and the like.

BAUBLES. My darling, where in the world did you learn that?   You're making my heart go pitty-pat with all that techno jargon....get down here and dance with me!

CHAOS. She has no idea what she's talking about...[*To VAGUE.*].. do you?

VAGUE. No.

CHANCE. Enough!   Are you going to help me clean up or not?   I can't possibly do everything by myself.   [*Indicating a broom leaning against the wall.*]   Chaos, man that broom.   Clean up your 'decorating'.

CHAOS. [*Tentatively takes the broom but instead of sweeping, leans on it.*] And what if we don't like them?   Then we'll have done all this work for nothing.   You know what a mess it makes when we have to drive them away again....

CHANCE. It's just a chance we'll have to take.

VAGUE. No, no, please don't say we won't like them, Chaos.   I want to like them.   I want them to like me....

BAUBLES. Don't be such a baby, Vagee-poo.   Remember the church people?   You said they gave you a skin condition.   You couldn't wait for them to leave.

CHAOS. They were like digging a splinter out of your finger.   It took forever and it hurt like h...

VAGUE. Chaos!   Language!

CHAOS. Well it did.   But like the splinter, it felt so good to get them OUT!   They were so sanctimonious.   All that bible thumping made my head hurt.   Let me tell you, when I was done with that preacher, he was a true believer.   [*Arms raised and with the motions of a evangelistic preacher on his pulpit.*]   Yes, sir, A. TRUE. BELIEVER.

[*ALL laugh at the memories.*]

BAUBLES. Oh, Chaos, you are such a naughty spirit.... [*Shaking HIS index finger in a 'shame on you' motion.*]   Naughty, naughty....

CHAOS. Well, I got rid of 'em, didn't I?

CHANCE. Yes you did. And for that I am eternally grateful.

BAUBLES. 'Eternally'? Oh, that's rich. [*Chuckling.*] 'Eternally'.

[A car engine is heard approaching. It stops and car doors are heard opening and slamming shut. Distant child's laughter is heard.]

VAGUE. *[Almost falling off HER ladder. SHE whispers.]* They're here! No, no this can't be happening. They're a day early. Oh, dear what will we do? The place is a mess!

CHANCE. Didn't I try to tell you? I said we had to....

CHAOS. Oh, shut up, Chance...

BAUBLES. Well, I for one don't care. If this lovely, old, antique of a lighthouse is good enough for Baubles, then it ought to be good enough for them.

> *[HE prances off and exits.]*

VAGUE. I'm hiding....I can't bear it...they won't like our lovely home...and they've got children....
[Sighing.] You know how much I adore children....

> *[VAGUE exits. VOICES are getting closer.]*

VOICES. *[Off.]* KATE, look at this view.
[Off.] Ben! Don't go too near the edge....
 [Off.] Oh, Rory, it's beautiful. Look at the color of the sea. Let's go inside and see the rest....

CHAO. Ugh! Kids! Did we know they had kids? I'm getting outta here.

> *[CHAOS exits.]*

CHANCE. Well, keep your fingers crossed. Maybe they'll like us....dirt and all.

> *[CHANCE exits. As the lights FADE, a creaking front door to the lighthouse begins to open.]*

KATE. *[Off.]* Oh, honey, look! It's absolutely perfect....

ACT I

Scene 2

Setting.   The living room in the lighthouse is bright and clean.

[KATE stands at the front window upstage. The sounds of a large truck is heard. SHE leaves the window, crossing to an interior doorway and shouts to BEN off stage].

KATE. Ben! They're here.

[BEN runs on, crosses to the window.]

BEN. Daddy's here! Already?
KATE. No silly. It's the movers. Daddy won't be here until later.
BEN. And he's bringing Claire...you promise?
KATE. Yes, darling. I promise. Claire's coming home. *[Crossing to the door.]*   Come on, let's get our things in here.   Did you finish cleaning your bedroom?
BEN. You bet. And I saw a big ship from my window, with lots of black smoke coming from the stacks. Mom! *[Imagination always in high gear.]* Do you think it's sailing to Hong Kong?
KATE. I don't know, sugar. We'll look it up on a map…once we find the maps.

[THEY cross and open the door to find MOVING MEN standing with THEIR arms full.]

MOVING MAN. Mornin', Missus. Where did ya want this?

[The MOVING MEN enter with a table, and sofa.]

KATE. Put the table under that window, just there. The sofa goes here.
[THEY exit and return almost immediately with a single bed.]
MOVING MAN. Which bedroom, Missus?
KATE. No, that goes under the large window here.
MOVING MAN. In here?
KATE. Yes, please. *[Looks at Ben and smiles.]* This way she'll have a gorgeous view of the coast...right, Ben?
BEN. Right!

> *[As THEY are moving furniture in and talking, CHAOS and BAUBLES glide in. BEN is the only one who sees them and is visibly shaken but intrigued.]*

BEN. WOW!

> *[BAUBLES quickly holds HIS finger up to HIS lips motioning BEN not to give THEM away.]*

KATE. *[To Ben.]* What sweetie?
BEN. Oh, nothing...I was just checking out the view again. It's RIDICULOUS!

> *[BAUBLES glides in and around the MOVING MEN inspecting the decor as THEY continue in and out with boxes, tables, chairs. KATE continues to direct THEM. CHAOS has moved to a corner to watch. BEN, his eyes popping out of his head sits down on the unmade bed and watches BAUBLES. No one is aware of the spirits except BEN.]*

BAUBLES. Really, Chaos, look at all this chintz...*[HE touches the sofa and matching chair and then sighs deeply, in despair.]* I suppose she has curtains to match...Ugh. A bed in the great room? How gauche. *[HE dances over to BEN.]* Who's the bed for?
KATE. *[To the MOVING MEN.]* That goes in the front bedroom, please.
[BEN opens HIS mouth to answer.]
BAUBLES. No, no, darling one, don't speak now...your Mum will think you've gone batty on her. *[In a conspiratorial whisper.]* We'll talk later.
[BEN's jaw snaps shut as HE stares.]
KATE. Ben...Ben! What in the world are you staring at? *[SHE laughs.]* You look like you've seen a ghost.

> *[BAUBLES and BEN speak simultaneously.]*

BEN. Nothing.
BAUBLES. We are not ghosts!
KATE. Wanna help me make up the bed? *[To the movers.]* Those go in the kitchen.

[Directing the MOVING MEN to put most of the boxes off stage. THEY cross and exit into other rooms.]

BEN. Sure.
KATE. Great. Find the box that says 'linens' and open it, will you?

[BEN looks through some boxes that have been left in the living room.]

BEN. Here it is, Mom.
KATE. Great...Find Claire's favorite sheets, will you, honey?
BEN. The purple?
KATE. Well... it's mauve...but yes, the purple ones. And the pillow cases with the violets.
BEN. Ewww. Girly.

[BAUBLES glides over and peers in the box as BEN brings out the mauve sheets and cases.]

BAUBLES. Oooo...Mag! Iced! *[To Ben.]* May I touch?

[BEN stares and nods. BAUBLES lifts the linens to his nose.]

Umm...they even smell of lavender. I adore bed linens...I wonder what count these are.....do you know, Ben?

[BEN shakes HIS head. KATE has escorted the MOVING MEN out the door and SHE exits with THEM.]

BEN. Want me to ask my Mom?
BAUBLES. No, best not. She might think it very odd, her son suddenly interested in high count cotton. Never mind. I just know these are Egyptian cotton. Whose Claire?
CHAOS. Probably another kid. Just what we need.

[BEN stars at CHAOS.]

BAUBLES. Cat got your tongue, Benny?
BEN. My name's not 'Benny'. It's Benjamin. *[Shy.]* You can call me Ben.
BAUBLES. Of course I can. What a darling.
BEN. *[Awed.]* Am I the only one who can see you?
BAUBLES. At the moment.
BEN. Why can't my Mom see you?
CHAOS. Ha! That'd be a laugh. Adults running for their lives. Those burly moving men would scream like girls.
BAUBLES. Not a wise idea, Ben. Adults don't do too well with spirits.

BEN. Is that what you are? Spirits? Not ghosts.

CHAOS. Ghosts! Doesn't he know anything? Listen up, kid. Ghosts are unhappy things. Very gloomy. Now, spirits on the other hand are generally happy, and IF we like you, anything is possible.

[BEN turns back to BAUBLES.]

BEN. Why don't adults get to see you?

BAUBLES. We tried it a couple of times. It's impossible. They either want to drive us away with sage and crystals and Voodoo. *Or* they want to set up their little cameras, their special lights and sensor thingamajiggies, and then study us. We are not bugs! So we keep clear of the adults. Children on the other hand seem safer and braver somehow. Isn't that right, Chaos?

CHAOS. Yes. Just one drawback...they're kids.

BAUBLES. Who's Claire?

BEN. My sister. She's twelve.

CHAOS. Why does she need a bed in here? There are plenty of rooms.

BAUBLES. Chaos...please, your manners.

BEN. She's sick. My Mom says that she 'needs to be watched'. But I tried that once and Claire yelled at me.

CHAOS. Is it catching?

BAUBLES. Chaos...for Heaven's sake, what a thing to ask.

BEN. Do you guys live here?

CHAOS. I am not a 'guy'. Really!

BEN. I'm sorry. *[Beat.]* Are you sure you're not ghosts? That's what you look like.

BAUBLES. *[Laughing and prancing around the room.]* Ghosts! Goodness, no, what a thought. What a drab existence that would be. No, my dear, we're spirits. My name is Baubles and her name is Chaos. I'm a dancer, an entertainer...

CHAOS. Ha!

BAUBLES. *[Indicating CHAOS.]* And this rude thing is...she's... Well, she's Chaos.

BEN. Does that mean you cause trouble?

BAUBLES. *[Smirking at CHAOS.]* Ooo...smart boy.

CHAOS. Only if I'm provoked...which I frequently am, eventually...by children and preachers.

BEN. Oh. *[Beat.]* And you live here?

CHAOS. This is our home.

BEN. Cool.

BAUBLES. Very mag. Iced! And, to use your colloquial Americana, 'cool'.

BEN. *[Hoping the answer is 'yes'.]* Will you still live here, now that we've moved in?

CHAOS. That remains to be...

BAUBLES. Of course, we will, darling boy. And we can all be friends if you like.

BEN. That would be ridiculous!

CHAOS. *[Taking it literally.]* Yes, I quite agree.

BAUBLES. Don't pay any attention to her, Ben. She can be quite disagreeable.

CHAOS. What do you propose to do, Baubles, when he blabs to his Mommy that he is talking to a couple of wraiths?

BEN. Oh, I won't. I promise. I don't know what a 'wraith' is, but I promise not to tell.

BAUBLES. See, Chaos? We have his promise. *[CHAOS snorts.]* How 'bout this, Ben? For now you explain that you have imaginary playmates. Let's see, my name will be..

BEN. Henry.

BAUBLES. Hmm...Henry. Rather pedestrian but satisfactory. It couldn't be Hank, could it?

BEN. Henry. And... *[Indicating CHAOS.]* ...she can be Charlie.

CHAOS. A boy's name! No, absolutely not.

BEN. But, I wouldn't have a 'girl' imaginary playmate...

BAUBLES. Absolutely right. *[To CHAOS.]* Come on, 'Charlie', let's dash. See you later, Ben.

BEN. Later, alligator.

CHAOS. What? *[Feeling put upon enough for one day.]* Where!?

BAUBLES. Never mind, it's not a real alligator.

> *[BAUBLES pulls CHAOS off and as they exit, BAUBLES launches into the 'Purple People Eater' song from the fifties. KATE enters.]*

KATE. OK. Got the movers paid and on their way. Now, where were we?

BEN. I found the sheets and stuff for Claire's bed.

[BEN carries the linens over to the bed.]

KATE. Oh wonderful. What a big help you are. Let's get this made up for her, then we'll fix some lunch.

> *[BEN and KATE begin making the bed.]*

BEN. Can I have tuna fish?

KATE. *[Laughing.]* If I can find it, you can have it.

BEN. With the crusts cut off? Toasted?

KATE. If I can find the toaster, my man, you shall have a 'Ben's Special'. I'm glad we found the market on our way up...

BEN. Did you remember the...pickles? *[THEY speak* simultaneously.]

KATE. ...Pickles. Sure did. What's tuna fish without the pickles? **BEN**. A hot dog without the mustard!

> *[They begin a familiar game as the Scene ends.]*

KATE. A movie without the popcorn.

BEN. Bedtime without a story.
KATE. Oh, that's a good one! You win!

ACT I

Scene   3

Setting.   Claire's bed is made up.   There is a bedside table with a small lamp, a tray of medications, a couple of books and magazines, and a small pot of fresh flowers.   A car horn   sounds a merry message.

[CHAOS and BAUBLES are lounging on the sofa. KATE enters and crosses to the window.]

KATE. Ben! Ben, they're here.

[KATE rushes across the room to the front door and opens it.] Hello, darlings.[As KATE exits out the front door.]

Ben! Hurry, they're here!
CHAOS. [Bored.]   I guess they're here...
BAUBLES. Oh, goodie. Ben...

[THEY both turn expectantly to watch. BEN flies through the room and out the front door. Almost immediately RORY enters carrying CLAIRE who is their twelve year old daughter. SHE is draped in a light blanket. SHE wears a head scarf to hide her hair loss from chemotherapy. BEN is talking non-stop.]

BEN. I made your bed, Claire......well, I helped Mom make it. But I picked the flowers and Mom let me pick out the magazines to buy for you...How was the hospital this time?....[As Rory negotiates the doorway with his burden, Ben chatters on.]... Watch your head!!...How were the nurses this time? Did they take a lot of blood? Those are your favorite sheets, Claire...Mom thought...and Boy! Do I have something *awesome* to tell you!
RORY. Okay, son, let your sis get settled in....plenty of time to catch up later.

[During this, RORY has removed the blanket, removed Claire's slippers. KATE enters carrying a small suitcase. SHE takes over getting CLAIRE into the bed.]

KATE. Okay, sweetness, let's get you tucked in. I made soup for lunch and then maybe a little nap after?

[BAUBLES and CHAOS rise and move stage right.]

CLAIRE. I'm not really very hungry, Mom.
KATE. *[To CLAIRE as SHE carries the case over to the doorway to the bedrooms.]* I'll unpack your suitcase later, honey. Anything you need out of it right now?
CLAIRE. My book, please.

[As KATE retrieves the book and crosses to Claire, BEN bounces up on the end of CLAIRE's bed.]

BEN. How do you like the lighthouse? It's the coolest, right? Boy! Do I have a surprise for you! *[Bouncing up and down.]* Wait 'till you meet Henry and Charlie.
RORY. Not now, Ben.
CLAIRE. That's okay, Dad. I've missed the little beast. *[To BEN.]* Who's Henry and Charlie? Some kids in the neighborhood?
BEN. No. You'll see. Just wait.
KATE. *[Putting her arm around RORY.]* Help me in the kitchen, will you darling?
RORY. Sure thing. Be right back, you two. Don't wear your sister out, Ben.

[KATE and RORY exit. CHAOS AND BAUBLES wander over to the bed.]

BEN. *[Whispering to Claire, even though CHAOS and BAUBLES are right there.]* Can you see them?
CLAIRE. *[Whispering back.]* Yes....who are they?...*[Beat.]* What are they?
CHAOS. *[Indignant.]* We can hear you, you know.
BAUBLES. *[To Chaos.]* Quiet. *[To Claire.]* Hello, Claire. We're spirits who have had the honor....to be chosen...
CHAOS. Here we go....
BAUBLES. ....by Ben here, to be his imaginary playmates. I'm Baubles and this is my dubious friend, Chaos.
CHAOS. And I'm not anybody's 'playmate'.
CLAIRE. *[In awe.]* Are you real?
BAUBLES. Oh, yes, darling girl, very real.
BEN. Wait 'till you see one of Baubles' Lisa Macaroni's *[Mispronouncing it 'Lisa' instead of*

'Liza'.] dance numbers...
BAUBLES. Lisa Minnelli.
BEN. Yeah, her.... and you'll see how real they are.

> *[Beat. Pointing to CHAOS and BAUBLES are if THEY were exotic pets.]*

Aren't they *GREAT?*

CLAIRE. They certainly are. *[Claire holds out her hand.]* How do you do?
CHAOS. Very well all things considered.

> *[CHAOS ignores CLAIRE's hand. BAUBLES rushes in and takes her hand and gallantly kisses it.]*

BAUBLES. Enchant`e! We are delighted, simply delighted to meet you at last, ma jolie petite.
BEN. Oh! Before Mom and Dad get back, Clara-Bell....
CLAIRE. Don't call me that, brat. I am not a baby anymore and I am definitely not Howdy Doody's girl friend.
BAUBLES. Oh, I love that show. They never should have cancelled it....
BEN. Anyway *[long suffering.]*.....you gotta remember to call Chaos, Charlie and Baubles, Henry. That's who Mom thinks I'm talking to. You can call them their real names if Mom and Dad aren't around. Okay?
CLAIRE. I think I can remember that.
BEN. *You've got to.* Chaos says Dad will scream like a girl if he sees them....
CLAIRE. Okay. *[SHE points to Chaos.]* You're Chaos alias Charlie....and you're *[To BAUBLES.]* Baubles alias Henry. Hmmm...I think 'Hank' suits you better.
BAUBLES. *[To BEN.]* See? I told you. *[To Claire.]* That's what I thought. 'Hank' has a touch of swash-buckling, don't you think?
CLAIRE. Definitely.
BAUBLES. We are going to get along famously, darling Claire.

ACT I

Scene 4

Setting. The Lighthouse. A week later.

*[Claire appears pale but HER spirits are upbeat. CHAOS sits on the end of HER bed.
THEY are both laughing uproariously at something CHAOS has said.]*

CLAIRE. Baubles didn't... really...you're joking with me, right?
CHAOS. Would I joke a sister? Cross my heart.... *[Makes the motion of crossing her heart; but
leaves out the "hope to die".]* Baubles did this fabulous rendition of Cyd Charisse in front of three
hundred businessmen from Atlanta and not one of them knew that she wasn't a girl....

[A beat or two of CLAIRE and CHAOS looking at each other.]

CLAIRE. Why are you being so nice to me, Chaos?   I thought you didn't like kids.
CHAOS. The jury is still out...but at least you're a girl.   Ben's okay for a boy but he's still sweaty
and noisy most of the time.
CLAIRE. *[Very serious.]* It's not because I'm....sick, is it?
CHAOS. Sick? Are you sick? *[Laughing.]* Like in mental?
CLAIRE. *[Can't help but laugh too.]* Nooo....not 'mental'. You're the one who's mental around
here.
CHAOS. Ha! I'm the sanest spirit you have ever met. Admit it!
CLAIRE. You and Baubles are the only spirits I've ever met, wha'd ya talkin' about? *[Beat.]* But,
be serious. Please don't be nice to me because I have cancer, okay? I get that all day. You should
see them at the hospital. They treat me like I'm made of glass or something.
CHAOS. Absolutely not. For a kid, you ain't so bad and...well, I didn't have any 'chaos' scheduled
this afternoon so here we are....

CLAIRE. You promised me the next time you had time you would tell me a story about this old lighthouse.

CHAOS. Oh yeah. Let's see....I know just the one....but after the story you gotta promise to take a rest.

[CHAOS straightens the covers and tucks CLAIRE in. CLAIRE snuggles down amongst HER pillows.]

CLAIRE. Okay. Deal.

CHAOS. Okay. Well, this was about seventy-five years ago and....

CLAIRE. Jeesch! How old are you?

CHAOS. Never mind, a lady never reveals her age. *[Beat.]* The lighthouse was active then and manned by the Coast Guard. The crew consisted of about eight guys. They were the cutest boys ever. *[Beat.]* One night it was storming to beat all. My Coasties were right here in this very room playing poker and drinking beer. After a couple of hours of cards, they thought they heard a voice crying but it sounded more like the wind outside so they didn't pay much attention. Chuck, one of my favorites, by the way,...was sitting facing the window. Suddenly he jumps up, knocks his chair over, spills his beer, and points at the window. He turns white as a ghost, *[Chuckles.]* no pun intended, and can't talk. His buddies start razzing him about not being able to hold his beer and to sit down and play. Well, Chuck keeps pointing at the window and sort of gagging. *[Beat.]* Have you noticed that adults don't do so well when they see something that isn't supposed to be there?

CLAIRE. Yeah, tell me about it. You know, like my Dad. He refuses to believe that I'm sick..that I might, well you know...die. He keeps pretending that all I have is like a head cold.

CHAOS. I know, Baby-girl. But, let him pretend. He's just very worried. He loves you so much. *[Beat.]* So! Where was I?

CLAIRE. Chuck and the window....

CHAOS. Exactly. So a couple of other guys turn around to look where Chuck is pointing and they about fall out of their chairs. *[Laughing.]* In the window is an old fisherman, dressed head to toe in Sou'wester's...

CLAIRE. Sow...what?

CHAOS. Sou'wester's....yellow slicker rain gear that fishermen wear in bad weather. Anyway, this old guy is motioning for them to come. Well, my boys are scared out of ten years of growth, believe me.

CLAIRE. Was it a spirit?

CHAOS. Naw. Just a ghost. A spirit would've marched in here and gotten their attention quick. Ghosts are sort of shy and sad.

CLAIRE. So what happened?

CHAOS. The voice got louder and now my boys knew it wasn't the wind. The ghost disappeared from the window. Well, Chuck tells the other guys he's going out to check and who's going with him? Not to be outdone by him, the boys get into their foul weather gear and go to investigate. Once they get outside, the voice is louder.

They grabbed their rescue gear and headed down to the dock...

CLAIRE. There used to be a dock?

CHAOS. With an open sea rescue boat. They all piled into the boat and headed out. And guess what they found?

CLAIRE. What?

CHAOS. A young fisherman hanging onto a life ring. His boat was already gone. When my boys got to him, he was just seconds from drowning.

CLAIRE.*[Excited.]* Did they rescue him? What about the ghost? What happened?

CHAOS. Yes, my boys snatched him out of the bowels of that storm just in time. And the ghost, well, let me just say this....the fisherman that they rescued looked exactly like a younger version of the face at the window....

CLAIRE. Cool.

CHAOS. O.K. Story over.

[Tucking CLAIRE's covers around HER.]

Close your eyes and get some rest.

ACT I

Scene 5

Setting. The Lighthouse. A lazy Sunday afternoon.

[KATE and RORY are in the living area playing scrabble with BEN. BAUBLES is leaning over BEN's shoulder watching. HE is helping BEN form words. CLAIRE is sitting up in bed with a book in HER lap gazing out the window.]

BAUBLES. *[In a whisper to Ben.]* 'Ghost', you've got 'ghost' for thirty points.
BEN. Be quiet, Henry. That's cheating if you give me words.

[KATE looks past BAUBLES as SHE refers to BEN's friend.]

KATE. That's right, Ben.   *[To the air where she thinks Henry is.]*   You can't help make up words, Henry. That's cheating.

[BAUBLES flounces down on the floor and pouts.]

RORY. Ben, how long has Henry and Charlie been around? Did you play with them at our other house?
BEN. Yeah, that's where I met them...ah...at our old house...
BAUBLES. Naughty, Ben. You shouldn't tell your Dad a lie.
BEN. *[To BAUBLES.]* Quiet! It's not polite to interrupt.
RORY. Is Charlie here too?
BEN. No, he had to go home to go shopping with his Mom...
BAUBLES. Oppsy! Another big whopper!

CLAIRE. Mom, someone's coming.
KATE. *[KATE rises and crosses; looks out the window.]*
Hmm....wonder who that is.

[BEN and then RORY cross also. BEN bounds up on the bed to get a better view.]

BEN. What kinda car is that, Dad?   It's really old.
RORY. That, my fine friend, is a 1959 Edsel station wagon.....a classic.
BEN. It's goofy lookin'.   How old is that thing?
KATE. Do the math, Ben.
BEN. Two thousand eight take away nineteen fifty-nine...Wow! That car's forty nine years old....the lady's got a basket, Dad.   Maybe with cookies....
 RORY. *[Laughing.]* We can only hope, son.

[As they talk, BAUBLES has risen and crossed over to lean on CLAIRE's headboard.]

BAUBLES. What's all the fuss?   *[Looks out window.]*   Oh, no! Not them again!

[BAUBLES whirls and rushes off.]

Chaos!   Chaos!   They've come back.....the Tuttles are here.....
KATE. Ben, put the game away....looks like we have company.
BEN. *[Grumbling.]* But, Mom, I was winning.

[KATE and RORY cross to the door and open it as the doorbell rings. REVEREND and MRS. TUTTLE walk in on the next lines. REV. TUTTLE is loud and obnoxious. MRS. TUTTLE is a mouse.]

REVEREND TUTTLE. Afternoon, my good people! Lovely day isn't it?   I'm the Reverend Tuttle and this is the wife.

[Shoving HIS hand out to RORY. TUTTLE is loud and jolly.]

You must be Mr. Fuller...and   *[Taking KATE's hand next.]*   ...this here must be the little woman. How do you do?

[RORY and KATE are speechless. The REVEREND turns to BEN.]

Now, who's this big strapping lad?
BEN. *[Very quiet, polite.]*   Benjamin, sir.
REVEREND TUTTLE. How-de-do.   *[Ruffles BEN's hair.]*   Yes, sirree, a fine boy.

[The REVEND goes quiet as he spots CLAIRE.]   Ah....this must be…Ah...your daughter…Clara.

[KATE, speechless to this point, finally comes to.]

KATE. *[Correcting HIM.]* Claire. You know my daughter, Reverend Tuttle?
REVEREND TUTTLE. No, no... just heard about the poor unfortunate...
KATE. *[Interrupting HIM.]*   Won't you sit down? Can I offer you and Mrs. Tuttle some tea?
MRS. TUTTLE. That would be lovely, dear, thank you.
KATE. I'll be right back.

[KATE exits to the kitchen, BAUBLES and CHAOS enter. They stand together, and KATE almost walks through them. They part at the last moment. RORY escorts the TUTTLES to the sofa.]

CHAOS. *[To BAUBLES.]* I prayed that you were joking....
BAUBLES. I never joke about the Tuttles.
BEN. Sir, is your car really forty nine years old?
RORY. Ben...
REVEREND TUTTLE. No, no, Rory...may I call you 'Rory'? It's a perfectly good question. Yes, Benjamin, it's a classic, you know. Had it since 1978.   Only twenty five thousand miles on it when I bought it. Runs like a top.
MRS. TUTTLE. *[Very tentative.]*   The Reverend's congregation has offered to buy us a new....
REVEREND TUTTLE. Now, Missus, you know I couldn't allow that....besides that car is my pride and joy. God forgive me for the mortal pride a man feels about his 'wheels', right, Rory?
RORY. It's a beauty, Sir.
[KATE enters with a tea tray. SHE crosses to the coffee table and begins to pour tea.]
KATE. Ben, get some milk for you and your sister, will you, dear?
BEN. Sure.

[BEN crosses and as HE starts to exit. BAUBLES stops HIM and during the dialogue between THEM, the TUTTLES and RORY and KATE are quietly talking.]

BAUBLES. Ben! Do you know who that is?
BEN. Yeah...some reverend guy. He's got a really old car that he's proud of. I don't get it...
[BEN exits.]
CHAOS. We'll just have to handle this ourselves.

[CHAOS starts to march over to the TUTTLES.]

BAUBLES. Wait a minute, Charlie.
CHAOS. Don't call me that!
BAUBLES. *[Grins.]* Alright, don't get your shroud in a knot. *[Beat.]* Maybe they'll drink their tea and go away. Let's wait.
CHAOS. Ha! Fat chance.

> *[CHAOS leans against the wall, observing. BAUBLES crosses behind the sofa and leans in between REV. TUTTLE and MRS. TUTTLE.]*

 RORY. So, Reverend Tuttle, which church is yours?
REVEREND TUTTLE. *[Pompous.]*   The Blessed Church of the Sacred Blood of the Precious Lamb, sir. Out on Old Town Road.
RORY. Hmm...can't say that I know it.
BAUBLES. *[Even though RORY can't hear HIM.]* That's because the guy's a hack, Rory.
CHAOS. He can't hear you, *Hank!*
REVEREND TUTTLE. It's a modest little building...
MRS. TUTTLE. You must come to service some....
REVEREND TUTTLE. Please, Missus, not when the men are talking.
MRS. TUTTLE. Excuse me, Reverend.
REVEREND TUTTLE. You'll have to come worship with our little flock soon, Rory. You and your family. Is your daughter ambulatory?
RORY. *[Clinching HIS teeth.]* Yes Sir. She's also right here in the room, Reverend.
REVEREND TUTTLE. *[Puts his hand on Rory's shoulder.]* Yes, of course she is, my son. Just remember that Our Lord never gives us a burden so heavy that we cannot carry....
KATE. *[Cutting in quickly.]*Sugar or milk, Mrs. Tuttle?

> *[Sighing, BAUBLES wanders away, crossing to CLAIRE and picks up a magazine.]*

MRS. TUTTLE. Just a little sugar, please, Mrs. Fuller.
KATE. Reverend Tuttle? Tea?
REVEREND TUTTLE. Nothing, thank you.
KATE. Coffee perhaps?
REVEREND TUTTLE. I don't imbibe in stimulants, Missus.   Just God's pure, sweet water is good enough for me.   *[Beat.]*   Mrs. Tuttle, on the other hand, cannot seem to give up her tea. *[To Mrs. Tuttle.]* Missus, didn't you bring an offering?

> *[MRS. TUTTLE has been sitting with HER basket on HER lap.]*

MRS. TUTTLE. Oh! Yes. Mrs. Fuller, I brought you a little house warming gift.
[SHE passes the basket to KATE.]
RORY. I think I'll get a beer. Can't stand tea. *[HE exits.]*

REVEREND TUTTLE. Ahem.....it *is* the Sabbath....

KATE. *[SHE addresses the gift basket.]* How lovely, thank you.   Look, children, cupcakes.

[BEN enters carrying two glasses of milk. HE crosses and gives one to CLAIRE.]

BAUBLES. *[To BEN.]*   Where's mine?

BEN. *[Giggling.]*   Henry, you don't drink milk.

BAUBLES. *[Mimicking the Reverend.]*   '.....the Lord's pure sweet water is good enough for me....'

BEN. Shh.. *[Forgetting that the adults cannot hear the spirits.]*..he'll hear you.   What're you reading? *[Gets a look at the fashions.]*   Ugh! Girls' dresses.....again?

BAUBLES. This is Vogue, Ben. *Vogue.*

CLAIRE. Yeah, so buzz off, beast.

[Leaning over CLAIRE's magazine.]

BEN. But why are their eyes all black? Why are they so skinny? What happened to their hair? It's gross.

BAUBLES. They are not 'gross'. They're haute couture models.

BEN. I don't care. They're ugly, Henry. *[BEN crosses to the cupcakes.]*

REVEREND TUTTLE. *[Hearing Ben's side of this conversation.]* Who is your son speaking of? Who's Henry?   Do you have another son?

KATE. No, Henry is Ben's imaginary playmate.

MRS. TUTTLE. How sweet...

[The REVEREND gives her a hard look.]

REVEREND TUTTLE. Really, do you think that's healthy? You know you have to always be alert to the devil's ways.

   KATE. *[Jumps in again.]* Yes, it's perfectly healthy, Reverend, for a boy Ben's age who has moved to a new place and hasn't met any friends yet to create a playmate.

REVEREND TUTTLE. Of course, my dear. I am only concerned for his soul.

[RORY enters. Sensing HE's missed something big, HE grins and winks at BEN.]

KATE. His soul is perfectly safe, I assure you Reverend Tuttle. *[Beat.]*   So, Mrs. Tuttle, do you have children?

MRS. TUTTLE. No, unfortunately. The Lord's not blessed us....

CHAOS. The Lord in his wisdom, she means....

KATE. *[Handing BEN a plate.]*   Ben thank Mrs. Tuttle for the lovely cupcakes.

BEN. *[Taking the plate, he mumbles his thanks.]* Thank you.

MRS. TUTTLE. What a charming child. Benjamin, I see you have two teeth missing. Did the tooth fairy leave some money for you?

 BEN. *[HE points to a missing tooth.]* Yes, Ma'am, for the first one he left a dollar.

MRS. TUTTLE. And the second one?

BEN. A gold coin.

MRS. TUTTLE. Oh my. The tooth fairy left you gold?

BEN. No, Ma'am, it was pirates.

MRS. TUTTLE. *[Chuckling.]* Oh, my.

KATE. *[Handing BEN a plate.]* Ben, will you take this over to your sister?

CLAIRE. No thanks, Mom. I'm not hungry.

BEN. Can I have hers?

REVEREND TUTTLE. Gluttony is not a virtue, my young man.

KATE. *[Glares at TUTTLE.]* Finish that one first, okay, Benny?

BEN. No, I mean another one for Henry.

KATE. Oh, sorry. Of course. *[Puts one on a plate and hands it to Ben.]* Here you go.

[KATE and BEN grin at each other. BEN crosses to the bed. BEN keeps the plate and cupcake but BAUBLES gleefully breaks off pieces and eats it.]

REVEREND TUTTLE. So...Rory....Mrs. Fuller...

KATE. Please call me Kate.

REVEREND TUTTLE. Yes, thank you, Kate. I have heard about your daughter...ah... *[Forgetting her name.]*

RORY. Claire.

CHAOS. Look at that, he can't even remember Claire's name...

CLAIRE. Its okay, Charlie, I don't care...

REVEREND TUTTLE. Yes, yes indeed. Claire. Her unfortunate illness. *[HE whispers.]* We understand that it is very serious...terminal?

[CHAOS jumps up and starts across to the REVEREND.]

CHAOS. That's it! How dare he? The wind bag cannot talk about our Claire as if she isn't here... *[BAUBLES leaps off the bed to restrain CHAOS.]*

 BAUBLES. Just wait. I have a little surprise planned. Just be patient. You'll like it I promise.

CHAOS. Okay. But, it had better be good. *[Beat. BAUBLES grins at CHAOS.]* Okay, you get the good Reverend. I get Mrs. Reverend.

BAUBLES. Fair enough.

KATE. *[Shocked at the REVEREND's crassness.]* With all due respect, Reverend Tuttle, we do not use those words in my house. Claire is ill but she'll make a complete recovery. Just as soon as we get the bone marrow match.

MRS. TUTTLE. *[Equally distressed.]* My dear Kate, Reverend Tuttle meant no harm....he just meant...that is....

REVEREND TUTTLE. Mrs. Tuttle, please. I am capable of explaining my meaning....I do not need your assistance.

[CHAOS snaps HIS fingers in front of MRS. TUTTLEs face.]

MRS. TUTTLE. *[Completely out of character, SHE becomes someone else.]* Well, really, Howard, how crass can you be?   The child's right here in the same room with us. Really! What in the world are you thinking?

REVEREND TUTTLE. MRS. TUTTLE! Be Quiet! You question me? The truth is the truth. *[Changing his demeanor, he turns to Kate.]* My dear woman, I meant no harm. I merely wanted to offer our assistance and let you know that we that is Mrs. Tuttle and I and our whole congregation are praying for you and your daughter.

KATE. Thank you, Reverend. We appreciate your prayers.

RORY. You need to understand that Claire will get well...she's getting better every day. *[Looking over at Claire.]* Aren't you, baby?

CLAIRE. Sure, Dad.

REVEREND TUTTLE. Might we pray with you and your family, Kate?   Prayer is the most powerful thing when two or more Christians gather....

KATE. *[Mollified.]* A little prayer can't hurt.

RORY. Oh, I don't know....

BEN. *[Whines.]* Do we have to?

BAUBLES. *[To the room in general.]* Oh, darlings, here he goes again. Don't do it, Kate.

[Even though KATE cannot see or hear HIM, HE flutters around her.]

You don't have to do it, Kate. He's just an old windbag.....

KATE. I appreciate your trying to help. But, please don't be too long. Claire usually naps in the afternoons.

BAUBLES. *[Still fluttering right in KATE's face.]* You don't know what you're getting us all into, Kate....

CLAIRE. She can't hear you, Hank.

BAUBLES. Then I shall just have to take charge.   Never let it be said that I didn't warn the good Reverend the last time he tried this.

BEN. What're you gonna do, Henry?

BAUBLES. Watch and learn, grasshopper.

REVEREND TUTTLE. *[TUTTLE rises and crosses towards CLAIRE'S bed.]* Wonderful! If we could just gather around the sick bed....

[EVERYONE rises, with different degrees of enthusiasm and cross to CLAIRE's bed. CHAOS and BEN sit on the end of the bed. KATE takes CLAIRE's hand.

RORY stands behind the headboard.]

CLAIRE. Mom.....do we have to?

KATE. The Reverend Tuttle is a guest in our home, Claire.   It's very kind of him. *[KATE leans in and whispers to Claire.]* Besides, after they leave, we have that wonderful chick-flick movie to watch.

REVEREND TUTTLE. Mrs. Tuttle, my Bible, if you please.

[MRS. TUTTLE takes a Bible out of HER large purse.]

MRS. TUTTLE. Here you are, Reverend.

REVEREND TUTTLE. Thank you, my dear.

[In an evangelistic, booming voice, the REVEREND begins praying.]

REVEREND TUTTLE. DEAR HEAVENLY FATHER!   WE ARE GATHERED HERE, IN YOUR NAME, TO ASK THAT YOU, IN YOUR INFINITE MERCY....

[The REVEREND lays HIS hand on Claire's head in a 'laying on of hands' gesture.]

HEAL THIS PRECIOUS CHILD OF HER DEADLY AFFLICTION......

BAUBLES. THAT'S IT!   That's enough....

[BAUBLES takes the flowing chiffon scarf from around HIS neck and passes it over the REVEREND. The theme song from Cabaret begins and the REVEREND launches into song and dance, but with flavors of evangelism. Prancing and dancing and singing across the room as if HE is a puppet. BAUBLES, the puppeteer, follows HIM and directs HIS dance steps with HIS hands.

REVEREND TUTTLE. *[Singing.]* 'What good is sitting alone in your room, come hear the music play....Life is a cabaret, old chum, come to the cabaret. Put down the knitting, the book and the broom, time for a holiday. Life is a cabaret, old chum, come to the cabaret....

MRS. TUTTLE. *[Eyes bugging out of her head, Mrs. Tuttle chases after him.]* Mr. Tuttle!

BEN. Iced! Maximum Cool!

KATE. Oh dear!

RORY. *[Trying hard to keep from laughing.]* You can say that again.

CHAOS. Perfection, Baubles. Pure perfection.

[REVEREND continues singing and dancing throughout the following dialogue.]

KATE. Maybe you should sit down, Reverend.

BAUBLES. *[Directing the REVEREND.]* Now...a little Buffalo shuffle back this way, Tuttle.

REVEREND TUTTLE. *[HE complies with a mix of cabaret dance steps with evangelistic energy.]*
'...come taste the wine, come hear the band, come blow your horn. Start celebrating...right this way,

your table's waiting...'
MRS. TUTTLE. *[Continues chasing the REVEREND around the room.]* Howard!

[The REVEREND prances over to MRS. TUTTLE and tries to dance with her. SHE immediately breaks away.]

MRS. TUTTLE. Really, Howard, calm yourself!
REVEREND TUTTLE. 'No use permitting some prophet of doom, to wipe every smile away, come hear the music play.   Life is a cabaret, old chum, come to the Cabaret!...'

[At BAUBLES' direction the REVEREND finally winds down and collapses on the sofa. HE returns to HIMSELF. BAUBLES spins away, laughing. CLAIRE and BEN hid their giggles behind their hands. The ADULTS are stunned.]

BAUBLES. Do we need more, Chaos?
CHAOS. Not if they leave within the next thirty seconds. Otherwise, let's hear some Judy Garland.

[CHAOS snaps his fingers in MRS. TUTTLE's face. SHE sits next to HER dazed husband.]

MRS. TUTTLE. Howard, REALLY!   Whatever is the matter with you? That was a disgraceful display....and on the Sabbath, to boot!
REVEREND TUTTLE. *[Reverend stares at her; not certain what happened.]* What are you babbling about, Missus?
KATE. Can I get him some water?
RORY. What happened?
CLAIRE. Henry and Charlie made him do a dance number for us. Better than prayers.
KATE. Henry and Charl...?
BEN. Wow!
REVEREND TUTTLE. Wha? What happened?   Martha?
MRS. TUTTLE. I cannot begin to describe your disgraceful behavior, Howard. What possessed you? Singing and dancing on Sunday?   What's gotten into you?

[BAUBLES, CHAOS, BEN and CLAIRE answer HER.]

CHAOS. Baubles!
BEN. Henry!
BAUBLES. Me! A little Lisa, compliments of Moi.
CLAIRE. Hank and Charlie!
KATE. That's enough, children.
MRS. TUTTLE. Please excuse my husband....I can't imagine....he's usually so proper...

KATE. Please, don't give it a thought, Mrs. Tuttle. Sometimes the.. *[Grinning.]* …spirit just moves us....

REVEREND TUTTLE. Mrs. Tuttle! I demand to know what everyone is talking about....I am the picture of decorum and respectability.   Why is everyone looking at me?

MRS. TUTTLE. It's all right, Mr. Tuttle. You just had a little spell. Everything is fine now.

REVEREND TUTTLE. But the prayer…we must pray over dear little Claire.

KATE. Oh, no, Reverend we already did that…right before your 'little spell'.

MRS. TUTTLE. Howard, I told you I thought this was a bad idea. Considering what happened the last time we visited this dratted lighthouse.

REVEREND TUTTLE. Nonsense, my dear.

MRS. TUTTLE. Say what you will; I *still* think it's haunted.

[BAUBLES and CHAOS float around MRS. TUTTLE making 'ghost' sounds.]

CHAOS. Ooooooo…..

MRS. TUTTLE. It gives me goose-bumps just being here.

BAUBLES. *[Tugs at a strand of HER hair.]* Boo!

[MRS. TUTTLE swats at HER head as if swatting a fly. BEN giggles. CLAIRE laughs   out loud.]

MRS. TUTTLE. Eek! *[Beat.]* We should be going, don't you think?

REVEREND TUTTLE. Whatever you say, dear Martha. We do have other calls to make.

MRS. TUTTLE. *[SHE turns to Rory and Kate.]*   I believe it's best if we go home now and let Mr. Tuttle rest.

REVEREND TUTTLE. But...

MRS. TUTTLE. Don't argue, Howard. I know best in this situation. You're not yourself. Now....*[Helping HIM up.]*   ...up you go.

[THEY cross to the front door.   The REVEREND stops by CLAIRE's bedside.]

REVEREND TUTTLE. My dear child. I hope that our prayers helped you.

[BEN, CLAIRE, BAUBLES AND CHAOS all giggle.]

CLAIRE. Oh yes, Reverend Tuttle, your 'prayer' *[Referring to the dance number.]* was the best I've ever seen....umm...heard. Thank you.

REVEREND TUTTLE. Well, that is most gratifying....Would you like one more before we depart?
     [Everyone speaks simultaneously.]

KATE. No!

MRS. TUTTLE. No!

RORY. That won't be necessary.

BEN. Oh! Yes, please.

CLAIRE. Oh, dear no, I think one is all I can take in one afternoon. I'm very tired.

CHAOS. *[Warning.]* He's not gone, Baubles.

BAUBLES. *[Begins a countdown.]* Ten, nine, eight....

CHAOS. *[CHAOS gets right up to the REVEREND's ear.]*   Better hurry, you old wind bag...

BAUBLES. Seven, six, five...

BEN. Mom! Henry's doing a countdown.

KATE. What? Oh!

[Taking the REVEREND by the arm, SHE begins to quickly guide THEM to the door.]

Well, it was so good of you to come, Reverend. Mrs. Tuttle.

BAUBLES. Four, three, two....

[KATE is rushing THEM toward the door. RORY opens it and THEY push THEM out.]

KATE. *[To the TUTTLES.]* Thank you. Thank you. Good bye.

[THEY slam the door shut amidst much laughter.]

BAUBLES. One!

CLAIRE. Oh, Mommy, did you ever see anything like that, ever?

KATE. No, honey, I can't say that I have. *[SHE crosses to the sofa.]*

CHAOS. Brilliant! I must say, Baubles, you out did yourself!

[BAUBLES takes several bows with much flourishing.]

BAUBLES. Thank you. Thank you.

BEN. Will you teach me how to do that, Henry?

[As lights fade, KATE and RORY collapse on the sofa. BAUBLES and CHAOS sit on CLAIRE's bed, each picking up a magazine.]

BEN. I'm going outside to make sure they left.
        [HE exits.]

CHAOS. *[To Baubles and Claire.]*   Tell me again why you like these rags?

CLAIRE. *[Sighing she looks at Baubles.]*   She'll never get it.
BAUBLES. I know. I've tried.

INTERMISSION

ACT II

Scene 1

Setting. The Lighthouse. Several weeks later.

[KATE lies curled up on the sofa with BEN in HER arms. CLAIRE's bed is stripped of linens. BEN is crying.]

KATE. Benny, you mustn't cry so hard. You'll make yourself sick.
BEN. I can't help it, Mom, I miss her...
KATE. It's going to be all right, you'll see....
BEN. I miss Daddy, when's he coming?

[CHAOS AND BAUBLES enter. BEN takes no notice of THEM.]

CHAOS. What's happened? Why is Benny crying? What's going on?

[CHAOS whirls around the room, knocking things off tables. BAUBLES glides over to the sofa and tries to get BEN's attention.]

BAUBLES. Benny, what happened?
CHAOS. *[To BAUBLES.]* I. TOLD. YOU. We should never have left. Chaos reigns and I had NOTHING to do with it!
BAUBLES. Be quiet. *[Up close to BEN.]* Benjamin! Can you see me? Can you hear me?

[In HIS distress, BEN does not hear BAUBLES.]

CHAOS. *[Seeing the stripped bed.]*   Baubles....
BAUBLES. *[Ignores CHAOS.]*   Benny, please answer me.   What's wrong?
CHAOS. BAUBLES!
BAUBLES. WHAT?!
CHAOS. *[Pointing to the bed.]* Look!

> *[BAUBLES looks and rushes over to the bed. HE runs his hand across the mattress. HE then dashes back to BEN.]*

BAUBLES. Benjamin! Where's Claire's lovely Egyptian linens?   Where are the flowers? WHERE. IS. CLAIRE?

> *[BEN continues to ignore BOTH spirits. KATE continues to stroke HIS hair, trying to comfort HIM and HERSELF.]*

BAUBLES. *[Rushing back to the bed, Baubles throws himself onto it.]* Oh, no. Oh, no. It can't be.
CHAOS. I told you it was a bad time to leave. Didn't I say it was a bad idea?
BAUBLES. But, she was doing so well.   We weren't gone very long. Something's not right.

> *[On the sofa BEN has cried himself out and lies quietly. KATE is calmer.]*

KATE. Benny, are you hungry?   Want some lunch?
BEN. I guess so. When do you think they'll come back?

> *[CHAOS rushes over to BEN.]*

CHAOS. Who? What 'they'? Benny, I demand an answer!

> *[BAUBLES drifts over to the sofa.]*

KATE. Daddy didn't know. The hospital always keeps Claire for observation after her treatments. They wanted to test her production of cells again, see if anything has changed....

> *[CHAOS and BAUBLES stare at them and then stare at EACH OTHER. THEY grab each other in a hug and wild dance.]*

BAUBLES. Did you hear that?   She's not... *[Laughs hysterically.]*   She's just at the hospital again...she's not...
CHAOS. I have never been so frightened....not even when I was alive! *[Babbling incoherently.]* They said that they would give us a chance....and then to come home to this....

> *[BAUBLES breaks away and dances over to BEN.]*

BAUBLES. Benny?

BEN. Huh? Oh, hi, Henry. When did you get here? Why're you calling me Benny? You know I hate it.

CHAOS. *[Crossing over behind Baubles.]* Hey, kid!   What's going on? Can't we leave you for a minute?

BEN. Claire had a re--...are--...

KATE. Relapse.

> *[KATE looks on during BEN's conversation with HIS 'imaginary playmates'.]*

BEN. Yeah, a relapse. She had to go back to the hospital yesterday. She got pretty sick.

KATE. Ben, Are Charlie and Henry here?

CHAOS. Will she be back home soon?

BEN. *[Turning to KATE.]* Yeah. Mom, Charlie and Henry are worried about Claire. They want to know when Claire's coming home.

KATE. Tell them that we don't know for certain. Soon, we hope. *[Addressing Ben's worries.]* Tell them not to worry.

BEN. *[In a formal tone HE turns back to BAUBLES and CHAOS.]* Mom says not to worry. We don't know for sure but soon.

CHAOS. Yeah, we heard her, Ben.

BEN. Oh.

> *[As KATE and BEN continue to talk, BAUBLES AND CHAOS wander over to the bed and sit down side by side. THEY stare at the floor, dejected.]*

KATE. I've got an idea, Benny. Let's make some lunch....

BEN. Tuna fish.

KATE. Of course. By then the sheets will be done in the dryer. We'll make up Claire's bed just in case she gets to come home today. Then we'll take a nice long walk and find some wild flowers for her. How 'bout it?

BEN. Crusts cut off, toasted?

KATE. Absolutely….and pickles.

BEN. Pickles!

ACT II

Scene 2

Setting. The Lighthouse. A month later.

[CLAIRE has returned from the hospital. Lying in bed, SHE is pale and passive. SHE stills wears a head scarf. SHE appears to be sleeping. BAUBLES enters with a gift wrapped box. HE quietly settles on the foot of CLAIRE's bed. At the movement, CLAIRE opens HER eyes and gives HIM a weary smile.]

CLAIRE. Hi.
BAUBLES. Hey, there, girlfriend. What's shakin'?
CLAIRE. Not much. *[Beat.]*   I'm really tired.
BAUBLES. It was different this time, huh, kid?
CLAIRE. Yeah. They tried something new. Really knocked the stuffin' out of me. What's in the box?
BAUBLES. I made something for you. Wanna' see?
[CLAIRE perks up. SHE sits up and stuffs pillows behind HER.]
CLAIRE. Oh, yes, please.
[BAUBLES hands HER the pretty box. CLAIRE begins opening it.]
CLAIRE. *[Peeking into the tissue paper.]* Oooo....it's shiny.
BAUBLES. Open it...I can't stand the suspense.
[CLAIRE opens the tissue and takes out a shiny, sequined, outrageous head turban. SHE doesn't speak; just looks across at BAUBLES with tears in HER eyes.]
BAUBLES. Well, speak! Do you like it?

CLAIRE. Oh, Hank, *[CLAIRE sniffles.]* I adore it. It's beautiful!

BAUBLES. No crying! You'll get me started and then where will we be?

CLAIRE. You made it....for me?

BAUBLES. I did. *And,* I made one for myself so we can be twins.

[Pulling a similar one out of HIS pocket, HE arranges it on HIS head. Then HE reaches over and helps CLAIRE to put HERS on.]

BAUBLES. We are stylin' now, Sister-girlfriend. *[HE prances over to a small mirror on the wall and brings it back to CLAIRE.]* Here's a mirror, have a look at how beautiful you are.

CLAIRE. I love it. It's the most beautiful one I've ever seen. *[SHE preens in the mirror.]* Thank you, darling Hank.

BAUBLES. It was nothing....just a little something I threw together. You know Judy Garland wore turbans quite frequently, in later years. So did Joan Crawford and Betty Davis.

CLAIRE. I love your history lessons, *[Laughs.]* I know all about Judy Garland, but who's Betty Davis and Jane......?

BAUBLES. *Joan* Crawford....Oh, my darling, your ignorance is appalling! I must bring you my book on Old Hollywood. *[Sighs.]* Those were the days...talent oozing out of every pore of the greatest actors of that century. All you need today is a pretty face, a chiseled chin, great hair, big......, never mind....or who do you know....and ....Presto! You're a star. And more often than not, not an ounce of talent between all of them.

CLAIRE. What about Julia Roberts? Judi Dench? Nick Cage? John Travolta? *[Sighs.]* ....and Johnny Depp?

BAUBLES. I didn't say there weren't exceptions.

CLAIRE. *[Teasing.]* So you *do* think there is some talent after, oh say...1945?

BAUBLES. Very little, my darling. I will say the exceptions to the rule are glaring. But, back in the day, the talent abounded, flourished! Such style, such grace, such panache.

CLAIRE. What's 'panache'?

BAUBLES. It's a word that defies definition...you've either got it or you don't. *[Preening.]* I'VE. GOT. IT. *[Beat. Looks at CLAIRE in HER new turban.]* And, I dare say, YOU'VE. GOT. IT!

[CLAIRE looks at HERSELF again in the mirror.]

CLAIRE. I do?

BAUBLES. You most certainly do! With a capital 'P',..... PANACHE!

[As CLAIRE looks in the mirror, contemplating HER panache, BEN, KATE, with shopping bags, and CHAOS enter from the front door. KATE goes right to CLAIRE.]

KATE. Hi sweetness. Did you have a good nap? *[SHE kisses CLAIRE. Notices the new turban.]* Great head gear, where did you get it?

[BEN, CLAIRE, and BAUBLES all exchange looks.]

CLAIRE. Hank...I mean Henry gave it to me.

[ALL four now look at KATE to gauge her reaction. KATE crosses the room with HER bags and as SHE exits to the kitchen, speaks over HER shoulder.]

KATE. That's nice, dear. It's lovely....you're very beautiful. I've got to start dinner.
[KATE exits.]
CHAOS. I thought we agreed that there was to be no physical evidence of our presence?
BAUBLES. Oh, stifle yourself. It's only a hat. Kate didn't even blink.
BEN. It's really Mag, Claire. *[To BAUBLES.]* What makes it so shiny?
BAUBLES. Sequins, my little grasshopper. Hundreds of sequins. Hand sewn by yours truly.
BEN. *You* know how to sew? You're a guy!
CHAOS. *[To BAUBLES.]* Aren't you the little Suzy home-maker?
BAUBLES. Jealous, my darling? Want me to make you one?
CHAOS. Pleeese! *[Beat.]* How do you feel, Claire?

[BEN has joined BAUBLES on the foot of the bed. CHAOS leans against the head board, fiddling with CLAIRE's pillows.]

CLAIRE. Oh, so much better. Hank and I have been discussing old Hollywood. Did you know that at least three famous actresses wore turbans like mine?
BAUBLES. Each turban matched their ensemble of course.
CLAIRE. It was very 'panache'.
BEN. What's 'panache'.....sounds like a kinda' fudge.
CLAIRE. Well, little brother, it's hard to define. You've either got it or you don't. Hank says I've got it.
BAUBLES. *[Striking a pose.]* And, of course, I've got IT.
BEN. Do I get it?
BAUBLES. *[To save HIS feelings.]* No, dear, you're too young. You'll probably 'get it' when you're older.
BEN. Okay. *[Gets off the bed and crosses to kitchen door.]* All this talk about panache and fudge is making me hungry. I'm gonna go see what Mom's fixing for dinner. *[Exits.]*
CHAOS. I miss food....so much, I can't tell you.
CLAIRE. Oh! Poor Chaos...I never thought about it before. You and Hank don't need food, do you? How can you survive without Dr. Pepper?
BAUBLES. Ugh! Easy! Darling Clara-Bell, *[Claire shoots him a look.]* ...How can you drink that stuff...Gag!! *[HE falls over gagging.]*
CLAIRE. *[Laughing.]* It's the nectar of the Gods, Hank. It's an acquired taste. You don't really

have 'panache' unless you drink D.P.

CHAOS. You can keep your Carmelly sweet mess, little Claire.

CLAIRE. *[Laughing.]*   That's not even a word....

CHAOS. Who says?

BAUBLES. *[Sighing dramatically.]*   And they say I'm dramatic...

CHAOS. I would kill for fried chicken! Like my Mama used to make in an iron skillet. Mmm... And country gravy and grits and baby peas...and apple pie for dessert... Or a taco.

BAUBLES. Pleeeeze....my waistline is expanding just listening to you. I miss Beef Wellington, rare, asparagus el dente, a little wild rice, and a good Merlot. Perhaps a Cesar salad, hold the anchovies....

CHAOS. Baubles, you are such a peasant.......Cesar salad without anchovies?... just order the head lettuce with blue cheese and be done with it...

BAUBLES. It isn't a mathematical equation, Charlie, *[Taunting Chaos.]* It's a matter of taste. How can you drown out the fresh, crisp tang of the greens with fish... *[Turns to Claire.]*   I ask you, Claire darling, tell me. You, who are the picture of 'panache', cannot like anchovies.

CLAIRE. Well....umm...I do sorta like them......

CHAOS. A-hah!

BAUBLES. Wounded..I am mortally wounded! Claire! You betray me! Anchovies!   Really, it's too bourgeois!

CLAIRE. I'm sorry, lovely Hank...it's surely a matter of personal taste, isn't it?

BAUBLES. Oh, I suppose you're right.

CHAOS. Ah-hem....

BAUBLES.   *[Sputtering.]* Not a word out of you, you....you....self-satisfied, ego ridden, sanctimonious pipsqueak...

[CHAOS and CLAIRE burst into laughter.]

ACT II

Scene 3

Setting. The Lighthouse. Evening. A few days later.

[RORY sits on the sofa, head in his hands.   He is very still. KATE enters from the bedrooms, stops and observes her husband.   CHAOS and BAUBLES enter with HER and cross stage right.   THEY both observe the scene.   KATE then crosses and sits down beside RORY.]

RORY. How is she?
KATE. Tucked up in our bed....watching TV.   *[Beat.]*   Ben's conked out.
RORY. *[In a desperate whisper.]* How can you go on like this?   Acting like it's nothing more than a head cold.
KATE. It's all I can do....I can't...won't consider the alternative...
RORY. We have to.
KATE. Says who?
RORY. Says me.
KATE. She's going to get well. I won't even consider any other outcome.
RORY. *[Raises his voice.]* Oh, for Chrissakes, Kate, we're losing her.
KATE. Not so loud!
RORY. *[In a desperate whisper.]* WE. ARE. LOSING. HER.
KATE. No.
RORY. Yes. Get your head out of the sand, why don't you? Time is running out.
KATE. We are not...*will not*... lose her.   As soon as they find a match, she'll be home free. We just have to be patient.
RORY. For God's sake, Kate. THEY. ARE. NOT. FINDING. A. MATCH. We have to prepare ourselves.....for....*[HE breaks down, begins to weep.]*

KATE. Stop it!   What if she hears you?   Where is your faith?   We have to believe that she will get well.

RORY. I can't. My faith....it's gone...I don't believe in anything anymore. From the day my baby got sick....my faith just went away....

[RORY looks at KATE pleadingly tears running down HIS face.]

 I see her fading away....like a slow disappearing act. I can't see her..she used to glow...like there was a light inside her...all the time...I would be warm just being in the same room with her...Now, it's like a small candle sputtering out.

[As RORY continues, KATE becomes desperate.]

KATE. Stop it!   How can you?   She is not disappearing!
 CHAOS. Certainly not!
BAUBLES. No, she is not....!
KATE. I know she's ill....but she is *not* disappearing!

[RORY rises to HIS feet and begins to pace. HE becomes more and more angry.]

RORY. For sweets sake, Kate, get a clue. Our daughter is dying. There is no bone marrow transplant....there is no miracle... THERE. IS. NO. GOD. *[Beat.]* How can you pretend?   You're killing me with your positive attitude....all sweetness and light.... *[A stifled sob.]*.... You make me feel so alone.
KATE. *[Angry at last.]* Really?   You feel lonely?   And how do you think I feel...carrying this family, keeping the faith, keeping up appearances for Ben's sake when all the time I can see it in your eyes. Death...death for our child...our Claire...
RORY. *[Heated.]* That's not fair....

[BEN has entered on this last bit. HE doesn't understand; only hears the angry words.]

BEN. Mommy?

[RORY sits abruptly on the sofa. KATE crosses to BEN.]

KATE. Baby! What are you doing up?
BEN. I heard something....you and Daddy....are you mad at Daddy?
KATE. *[KATE gathers him up into her arms.]* No! I was just scolding him for eating all the ice cream. What a piggy!
        [RORY rises from the sofa and scoops BEN into HIS arms.]

RORY. Come on, Cowboy, saddle up....time for bed. *[As he starts to exit he turns to Kate.]* Be right back...... wait for me.

> *[KATE nods and sits back down on the sofa. CHAOS and BAUBLES follow RORY out. KATE sits quietly starring out at nothing. RORY enters again, CHAOS and BAUBLES follow close behind. RORY stops and watches KATE. BAUBLES blows on the back of RORY's head to get HIM to move and join KATE. BAUBLES and CHAOS cross and sit on the bed. THEY listen to RORY and KATE.]*

RORY. *[Rubbing the back of HIS neck.]* There's a draft in here. *[HE sits with KATE.]* I'm sorry...about before.

KATE. It's okay.

RORY. No, it's not okay. *[Beat.]* I said some things I shouldn't have. It's just that....I get so scared.

KATE. Me too.

BAUBLES. We all are.

CHAOS. Yes.

RORY. I know I haven't been there for you. You're right, you have carried us...all of us.

KATE. Rory...

RORY. No, please, let me finish. I haven't been much help to you....I know....I feel...I don't know...numb? Then I look at Claire and the reality comes crashing down. I want to run away, Kate.

> *[KATE takes HIM into HER arms.]*

KATE. Sweetheart....

RORY. When I have to take her back to the hospital...it's all I can do, not to run out of there, screaming......I keep thinking, what did I do?
Am I such a bad person that this is visited on my beautiful baby? My little girl.....it goes around and around in my head...what did I do to deserve this? Why can't it be me?

KATE. You didn't do anything.....she just got sick.....it's not your fault.

RORY. *[Voice trembling.]* What are we going to do?

KATE. I don't know.

CHAOS. *[Turning to Baubles.]* What *are* we gonna do?

BAUBLES. I don't know...

ACT II

Scene 4

Setting. The Lighthouse. A week later.

[CLAIRE is in HER bed and appears to be sleeping. KATE is curled up on the sofa weeping quietly. CHAOS sits on the foot of CLAIRE'S bed. BAUBLES is sitting at the foot of the sofa on the floor.]

CLAIRE. Mommy?
KATE. *[Quickly wipes her face of tears and tries to stop crying.]* Yes, darling?
CLAIRE. Mommy, don't cry.

[KATE rises and crosses to CLAIRE. BAUBLES rises and follows.]

KATE. Sweetheart, I'm not crying.
CLAIRE. Why are your eyes wet?
[Beat.]
KATE. Well, maybe I was crying a little bit.....but it's only because I'm tired.
CLAIRE. You mustn't be sad for me, Mom. Please don't cry.
[KATE sits on the edge of the bed and takes CLAIRE's hands.]
KATE. Oh, my darling girl, I'm not.
CLAIRE. Because it's going to be okay, Mom. Even if I die...it's going to be okay.
KATE. Sweetie, you're not going to die.
CLAIRE. I'm just saying....if I die....it's okay.
KATE. How...?
CLAIRE. Because I'm surrounded by angels....and they are protecting me.

KATE. Really? How do you know?

CLAIRE. I just do. *[Beat. Deciding whether to say more.]*   You know Benny's playmates? Henry and Charlie?

KATE. Yes...

CLAIRE. They're not playmates at all.

CHAOS. Oh, boy, here we go...

BAUBLES. Not a good thing to do, Claire....

CLAIRE. They're angels.

KATE. Claire....

CLAIRE. No, wait Mom. Let me tell you. They're my angels....sent to.....you know...to help me, guide me....

KATE. Henry and Charlie are really angels?

CLAIRE. Yes. Their real names are Chaos and Baubles.....they're spirits....angels...

KATE. Chaos and Baubles?

CLAIRE. But, don't tell Ben I told you. He's so proud of them. He's afraid if you knew you'd make him give them back.

KATE. *[KATE had to laugh.]* Give them back? To whom?

CLAIRE. Oh, I don't know. I don't even know where they came from. We had to give them names that you and Daddy would understand.... and we knew you would freak out if we told you who they really were....you know, spirits and all....so Ben pretends....well, we both pretend that they are his imaginary playmates.

KATE. And you think that they are.....

CLAIRE. Angels.

KATE. Yes....angels.....how long have they been here?

CLAIRE. Oh, forever. They live here.

KATE. *[Trying to take it in.]* They live here.

CLAIRE. Yes, here in the lighthouse. We're just the tenants....the lighthouse has belonged to them for centuries.

KATE. I see. *[Beat.]*   And you can see them?

CLAIRE. Oh yes!

KATE. Tell me more about them.

CLAIRE. Well, Chaos is...chaos... *[SHE laughs.]*....you know....very linear....but causes trouble...doesn't like kids very much....but says Ben and I have grown on her...she's very active.

KATE. She?

CLAIRE. Oh, yes, Chaos is a 'she'.   Very temperamental.

CHAOS. I am not!

CLAIRE. Yes, you are.

[CLAIRE sees HER mother looking around.] Chaos is arguing with me which she does a lot.

KATE. She's here? Right now?

CLAIRE. Oh, yes, they're here most of the time.

KATE. And....Baubles?

CLAIRE. He's adorable.

BAUBLES. Thank you.

CLAIRE. *[To BAUBLES.]* Well, you are.

KATE. And Baubles…..Is a she also?

BAUBLES. Perish the thought!

CLAIRE. Oh, no, he's a guy…..but he dresses like Lisa Minnelli and sometimes, if he feels like 'old, old Hollywood', Judy Garland. He's billed as a….*[Can't remember the expression.]*

KATE. *'Billed'?*

CHAOS. Drag Queen.

CLAIRE. ….that's it….'drag queen'. Thank you, Charlie.

BAUBLES. Please! Female Impersonator, to be exact.

KATE. Oh, honey, you're teasing me, right? This is out of some book you've read.

BAUBLES. Baubles is an original! I am not out of some book.

CLAIRE. No, Mom! That's why I'm not scared….'cause I know that Chaos and Baubles will take care of me…..no matter what.

BAUBLE. You've got that right, girlfriend!

[CLAIRE grins at BAUBLES.]

CLAIRE. If the transplant doesn't come through…..they'll help me to….you know… cross over…

KATE. Darling….you don't really believe that two angels are living here.

CLAIRE. Well, spirits, really…

KATE. OK…..spirits. But honey we don't know if spirits exist or not.

CLAIRE. Oh, but I do know. Baubles made me that wonderful turban…and you remember Reverend Tuttle?

BAUBLES. Don't go there, Clara-Bell….

CHAOS. Best leave that one alone, child….

KATE. Yes?

CLAIRE. Baubles made him do that crazy dance number. Remember? *[Laughing, turns to Baubles.]* Oh, Hank, that was wild!!

KATE. Hank?

CLAIRE. He doesn't like Ben's name for him….. *[Mimics BAUBLES voice.]* …'much prefers Hank;… it's more swash buckling.'

KATE. So, you are telling me that Hank….Baubles was responsible for that crazy Sunday afternoon?

CHAOS. I helped!

CLAIRE. Yes, Chaos, you helped. *[To KATE.]* Yes, Mom, aren't they the best?

BAUBLES. I love you too.

KATE. And Ben sees them too?

CLAIRE. Ben's the one who introduced me to them. *[Beat.]* They make me feel safe. So, you don't have to worry or cry or anything, Mom. I'm safe….and if I have to die…well, I have my angels to take me.

[KATE takes CLAIRE into HER arms and hugs HER. SHE gazes out.]

KATE. You are not going to die, my darling. We just have to hang on a little longer...just be patient...the bone marrow match is coming..I know it.
BAUBLES. That's right, dear Kate.
CHAOS. Hang in there…

ACT II

Scene 5

Setting. The living room is empty.

[CHAOS and BAUBLES are sitting on CLAIRE's empty bed, talking. Once in a while THEY look at something out of the window.]

BAUBLES. We've got to do more!
CHAOS. I know!
BAUBLES. She's giving up.
CHAOS. I know.
BAUBLES. She can't die!
CHAOS. I KNOW!
BAUBLES. Well, do something!

[As THEIR voices rise, BEN enters. BAUBLES pokes CHAOS to silence HIM. BEN crosses over to THEM and collapses on the floor by the bed.]

BEN. Hey!   Whach'a doin'?
CHAOS. Nothing.
BAUBLES. Just hangin' around doing spirit things.
BEN. Where's Claire?
CHAOS. Your mother bundled her up and took her to the cliffs. Claire wanted to hear the surf. *[Silence.]*
BEN. So.....what's goin' on? How come you guys aren't talking?

[BAUBLES and CHAOS exchange looks. CHAOS gives a slight nod.]

BAUBLES. We were talking.... about Claire.
BEN. *[Sad.]* Yeah.....she's getting sicker, isn't she.
CHAOS. A little, yes.
BEN. *This sucks big time!*
BAUBLES. Listen, Benny....you know how when we play 'War'?
BEN. Yeah.
CHAOS. Well, we're planning a strategy, just like in your game. But, you can't tell anyone, okay?
BEN. I would never!
BAUBLES. You've got to promise because we'll need your help with this. And if Kate and Rory find out...well...
CHAOS. Dire consequences, Ben. DIRE!
BAUBLES. You can tell them after.....but not before, okay. Promise?
BEN. Cross my heart, hope to die...*[Goes through the motions.]*   ....stick a needle in my eye.
CHAOS. Enough!   Little boys are so gruesome.
BEN. I'm not little. *[Beat.]*   So...what's the strategy?
BAUBLES. *[To Chaos.]* As I was saying, when Ben popped in, we have to do something! The petition isn't getting any results.
CHAOS. Petitions take time....you are so impatient!
BAUBLES. Excuuuuse me, but time and patience are something...

[Begins looking in HIS pockets, patting HIMSELF down as if looking for something.]

....we seem TO. BE. OUT. OF!
BEN. *[Eyes are round as he listens to them squabbling.]* What petition?
CHAOS. I am doing the best that I can.
BEN. What petition?
BAUBLES. Well, do better!   The high court....
BEN. What petition?
CHAOS. The high court has world matters to consider. They haven't gotten to Claire's case yet.
BEN. *[Yells.]* GUYS!
BAUBLES.CHAOS. What!?
BEN. What petition? What 'high court'?
BAUBLES. Chaos took Claire's case....
CHAOS. I'll tell him!
BAUBLES. Okaaay!   Do you always have to be so dramatic?
CHAOS. Benny! There's....
BEN. Ben. *[Correcting CHAOS.]*
CHAOS. Yes. Ben. Sorry.   There's a high court in our dimension. We took, well, *I* took a petition...
BAUBLES. I helped to write it.

BEN. When you were gone last week?

BAUBLES. Yes.

BEN. Is it like where God is?

BAUBLES. No, darling. This court is a low, high court. God is way up in the high, high court.

BEN. So who's in the low, high court?

CHAOS. This is never going to work.

BAUBLES. *[To Chaos.]* Quiet. Ben, picture your favorite show, Law and Order, right?

BEN. Yeah.

BAUBLES. That's a court show, right?

BEN. Well, part of it.

BAUBLES. Picture that part, okay?

BEN. Do they wear suits in the low, high court? Is there a judge and a jury?

CHAOS. Good grief.

BAUBLES. Not exactly. Anyway, Chaos went there and presented Claire's case.

BEN. *[Awed.]* Claire has a case?

CHAOS. Child, do you ever run out of questions?

BEN. *[Giggles.]* That's what Mom asks me all the time. *[Turns to BAUBLES.]* Does she? Have a case?

BAUBLES. Sort of. *[Beat.]* Hey! I've got an idea. Why don't you pretend that you are the judge and you sit here quietly and listen to all the evidence? How does that sound?

BEN. Sick! Am I a judge in the low, high court or the high, high court? **CHAOS**. *[At HER wits end.]* I don't care! You pick.

BEN. Does this mean you'll have to call me, 'Your Honor'?

BAUBLES. Yes, your Honor.

BEN. Totally ridiculous!

BAUBLES. Okay, your Honor. You listen to all of the evidence.

BEN. *[In HIS best judge-like voice.]* Proceed.

BAUBLES. *[To CHAOS.]* Well, genius? What do we do to speed Claire's case along?

CHAOS. The high court….

BEN. Low, high court.

CHAOS. Yes, Benjamin…

BEN. 'Your Honor'.

CHAOS. Sorry. Your Honor, thank you. *[To BAUBLES.]* Did you have to explain everything so precisely? *[BAUBLES shrugs.]* The low, high court said that they would get back to me.

BAUBLES. Not good enough. Claire doesn't have that much t….. *[Looks at BEN who is hanging on every word.]*   ….you know.

CHAOS. Our case is very strong. Once they get to it, I think it will turn out well.

[Totally out of patience, BAUBLES covers BEN's ears and explodes at CHAOS.]

BAUBLES. *[Yelling.]* *We don't have any time left!* SHE. IS. GIVING. UP.

CHAOS. *[Yells back.]* Don't you think I know that!?

[BEN peels BAUBLES hands off HIS ears.]

BEN. I can hear you guys, you know.   I got a question.
CHAOS. *[Ignoring Ben.]*   Now look at what you've done.
BAUBLES. I wasn't yelling, you were.
BEN. I got a question....
CHAOS. *[Yelling.]* I was not!
BEN. Guys....
BAUBLES. Were too...
BEN. Henry!   Charlie! Order in the court!
 BAUBLES. CHAOS. *[To BEN.]* What!?
BEN. How come you don't go to the high, high court? Go see God.

[CHAOS and BAUBLES star at each other, then at BEN.]

CHAOS. Oh, child, you don't know....
BAUBLES. Benny, it's not that simple...
BEN. Why not?
BAUBLES. Well, for one thing, it's God.
BEN. But I always thought that's what he's there for.
BAUBLES. *[In a whisper.]*   Do we dare?
CHAOS. *[In a whisper.]*   Do you think we could?
BEN. That's what I'd do....just like Law and Order....I'd go straight to the lady D.A. and make her listen to me.

[BAUBLES jumps off the bed, grabs BEN by the hands and whirls around the room.]

BAUBLES, Benny, my love, you are supremely *sick!*   So totally ridiculous I got chills. Lisa and Judy would be proud, proud, PROUD!

[CHAOS jumps in and joins the dance.]

CHAOS. 'Go see God'. Of course. You're brilliant, Benjamin!
BEN. 'Your honor'.
BAUBLES. CHAOS. Yes, Yes! Your Honor, you are brilliant!

ACT II

Scene   6

Setting. The living room is empty. A car is heard pulling up and car doors are slammed.

[KATE enters holding the door as RORY enters carrying CLAIRE. BEN follows.]

CLAIRE. Dad....I can walk. *[Rory starts to sit Claire on the bed.]*No, Dad, please. I want to be on the sofa.

[RORY detours and crosses to the sofa. Both PARENTS look shell-shocked and treat CLAIRE as if SHE is made of spun glass.]

KATE. *[As SHE takes Claire's coat and scarf.]* Are you sure, baby? You're still weak.
CLAIRE. Mom!....I'm sure. I don't want to be in bed anymore.
KATE. Ben, hang up our coats, will you baby?
BEN. Sure Mom.

[BEN exits with the garments. RORY has crossed to the bed and gotten a quilt which HE tries to cover CLAIRE with.]

RORY. How's that, sweetheart?
CLAIRE. Dad, I'm not cold....but thanks anyway.
KATE. Can I get you something, baby?
CLAIRE. I would love a D.P. *[Starts to rise.]* But I can get it.

RORY. No, sit tight. I'll get it. Katie, what can I get you?
KATE. Iced tea, please.
  [As RORY exits, BEN enters.]

RORY. On my way to the kitchen, Benny. Want something?
BEN. A coke, please Dad.
RORY. OK. Be right back.
[HE exits. BEN crosses to CLAIRE and sits with HER on the sofa.]
BEN. Are you really okay, Clara-Bell?
CLAIRE. I'm fine. *[She lightly punches her brother in the arm.]* And in honor of the occasion, I will ignore what you just called me.
RORY. *[Off.]* Katy......can you give me a hand?

  [KATE rises and exits the room.]

BEN. Are you really cured? *[Whispering.]* What happened?
CLAIRE. I'm not sure. I was real sleepy....they always give you 'happy juice'. That's what the nurses call it....it is sooo lame. They gave me a sedative before they took a new sample.
BEN. Of your bone marrow, right?
CLAIRE. Right.
BEN. How big was the needle?
CLAIRE. You are such a ghoul. Really big.....about as big as my arm. Now shut up.
BEN. Wow! Then what?

  [Unseen by the children, KATE and RORY enter and stand silently in the doorway, holding a tray with the drinks, listening.]

CLAIRE. Like I said, I was sleepy but I could still tell what the doctors were doing. I could hear them. But, I usually try to go away in my mind 'cause they think it doesn't hurt because of the sedative, but it does hurt a lot, so I go away.
BEN. Where do you go?
CLAIRE. My favorite place. Usually a beach somewhere....on a tropical island.
BEN. Mag! *[Beat.]* Then what happened?
CLAIRE. Well, this time the beach was sort'a weird. The sky was so blue it hurt my eyes and there was a sun and two moons up there all at the same time. The water was so clear you could see all the fish and the waves were all perfect.
BEN. Wow, I wish I could'a gone with you.
CLAIRE. Then the strangest thing of all.....Baubles and Chaos were there.
BEN. What!? Really?
CLAIRE. Really. They didn't talk to me or anything.
BEN. Bet that was hard for Baubles.

CLAIRE. *[Laughing.]*   Yeah. They just smiled at me and they took my hands and we went for a long walk down the beach. Then they walked me out into the waves and we swam around and we looked at the fish. I didn't need a snorkel or anything, I could just dive down and I didn't need to breath. It was real weird, but so wonderful. I felt like a mermaid.

BEN. That is so ridiculous!

CLAIRE. Then Chaos and Baubles were gone and I was swimming with two dolphins... they.....

BEN. What? What?

CLAIRE. The dolphins were smiling, just like at Sea Adventures. Of course, the dolphin that reminded me of Baubles was a complete show-off...walking backwards on his tail, jumping out of the water and doing flips.

BEN. *[In awe.]* I bet it *was* Baubles!

CLAIRE. The other dolphin kept squeaking at him, scolding, just like Chaos when they're here. *[Laughing.]* Then they were gone and I was suddenly sitting on the sand looking at the sea. I don't remember walking out of the water...all of a sudden I was on the beach.

BEN. Wow! That is way cool!

CLAIRE. Then I heard the nurses calling to me. I hate when that happens. I have to go back and sometimes I don't want to.

BEN. What happened next?

CLAIR. I woke up. And the doctors were there, looking at the chart and then they were all looking at me...kind'a weird...they were staring at me. Then they took a ton of blood *again*. It freaked me out.

BEN. *[Picking up the story from there. So awed, HE whispers.]* And then the cancer was gone?

CLAIRE. Yep.

BEN. Wow! How did that happen?

CLAIRE. I don't know. The doctors had the lab run the tests a second time and it was still gone.

BEN. I bet I know! Baubles and Chaos fixed you! The dolphins fixed you. They talked to God just like I told them to and you got fixed.

[CLAIRE leans down to BEN and whispers to HIM.]

CLAIRE. I think so too. But, don't tell Mom and Dad. They'll think we're….

[BEN and CLAIRE finish an often used sentence between THEM.]

BEN. CLAIRE.   ….certifiable, 'round the bend, wild and crazy, headed for the nut house, batty as a bed bug...*CRAZY!*

[THEY dissolve into hysterical laughter. CLAIRE starts to tickle BEN to make HIM laugh even more.]

BEN. Stop! Stop! I'm gonna wet my pants.

[BAUBLES and CHAOS enter. THEY are in diaphanous robes. Gone are BAUBLES' outrageous outfits. THEIR 'spirits' seem weaker.]

BAUBLES. What's all the hilarity about? Whad' we miss?
BEN. CLAIRE. Hi. You're back!
CHAOS. Hi yourself.   What's going on?
BEN. Claire's not sick anymore!   Her cancer went away.
BEN. You guys did it, didn't you? You fixed Claire. You went to the high, high court. *[Awed.]* YOU. WENT. TO. SEE. GOD! *[Silence.]*   Hey! Henry, why're you dressed like that?   Has Lisa or Judy seen you?   Lisa's gonna have a cow when she sees you dressed in that ugly robe.
CLAIRE. What's wrong? Hank? Charlie? How come you're all pale and stuff?

[BAUBLES and CHAOS sit with the kids. CHAOS takes BEN's hand and BAUBLES puts HIS arm around CLAIRE.]

CHAOS. Now listen. You mustn't get upset.
BAUBLES. We have to go away.
 BEN. No!
CHAOS. It's time...
BEN. But, I don't want you to...
CLAIRE. Why? This is so not fair....just when I'm getting well, you're leaving!?
CHAOS. Our job is done.
BEN. What job?
BAUBLES. Fixing Claire.
CLAIRE. You have to leave because you fixed me? I don't get it.
CHAOS. Remember, Benny, when I tried to explain the meaning of chaos and you insisted that there had to be a 'plan'? We argued for hours, remember?
BEN. Uh-huh.
CHAOS. Well, it turns out that you were right....much as I hate to admit it.
BAUBLES. Out of the mouths of babes.
CHAOS. *[To BAUBLES.]* Be quiet! *[To BEN.]* There is a plan, Ben. We thought, all of us, that we owned the lighthouse. My goodness, we were here long enough. But, it turns out that, according to God, we were.....
BEN. You went to the high, *high* court? YOU. REALLY. TALKED. TO. GOD?
BAUBLES. Well, Benjamin, it wasn't like we hadn't seen him before. We do get around, you know.
CLAIRE. Go on, what did you find out?
CHAOS. Well, as I was saying, according to God, there is a plan. We have been waiting all these centuries for *you*, darling Claire.
 BAUBLES. Yes, it was our mission. Only no one told us we had a mission. To think back on all those lonely decades, well centuries really, rattling around in this place, cut off from the bright lights, the music.

CHAOS. *[Interrupting.]* So, as I was saying....we were waiting for you.   We are your guardian angels and we were sent to help you.

CLAIRE. Oh, Hank! Charlie! I knew it! I just knew you were my angels. Was it you in my dream?

CHAOS. Yes, dear child, it was.

CLAIRE. And you became dolphins? Just for me?

BAUBLES. And it wasn't easy....let me tell you!   I kept getting water down my blow hole. Do you have any idea how much salt water burns when it goes down the wrong way?

CHAOS. Oh, for Pete's sake, Baubles, stop whining.

BAUBLES. *[Whining.]* Well, it did!

  BEN. How come you hav'ta go?

BAUBLES. Let's see....how do I explain this? We have to go and take a rest for a while. Until our next mission.

BEN. Like taking a nap?

CHAOS. Exactly…only longer than yours.

BEN. Then you get a new mission? Like James Bond?

BAUBLES. Exact-to-mundo, my little grasshopper!   But, sadly, no souped up, mag vehicles. No camera hidden in a ball point pen.....

CLAIRE. *[Reflective.]* So that's all I was, a mission?

BAUBLES. No, no, my darling Claire. You were so much more than that. Your health was perhaps a mission, but you? Never!   You were the best girlfriend ever. Your taste in haute couture is impeccable. You have panache. Judy, and Joan, and Bette are so jealous of your turbans. *[Beat.]* Oh! You will have hair! What color is it, darling?

CLAIRE. *[Can't help but laugh.]*   Light brown, like Dad's, last time I saw it.

[BAUBLES and CHAOS rise to say goodbye.]

CHAOS. Well, it's time.

BEN. No! NO! *[BEN throws himself into Chaos' arms.]* I don't want you to go.

[BAUBLES goes over to BEN.]

BAUBLES. Benny, it's okay. We won't be far away. You just won't see us. But, we'll always be around and we'll always be checking in.

BEN. You promise?

BAUBLES. Does a bear ......?

CHAOS. Really, Baubles, what would Kate and Rory think if they knew that you taught Ben those crude sayings?

BAUBLES. And if you ever really need us, we will be here in a flash....We'll have a secret signal, okay?

BEN. What is it?

BAUBLES. You start singing 'Over the Rainbow' as loud as you can....and I will come a-running.

BEN. You promise?

[BAUBLES and CHAOS cross to a wall and seem to slide right through and are gone. BEN starts to cry.]

CLAIRE. Benny, com'ere. Don't cry.

[BEN sits on the sofa and CLAIRE puts HER arm around HIM. KATE and RORY enter carrying the cold drinks.]

RORY. Drinks, anyone?

[KATE sits next to HER children.]

KATE. What's up, Buddy? Why the tears?

CLAIRE. Henry and Charlie had to go.

BEN. They left. *[Still crying.]* They're not coming back.

KATE. Oh, honey, I'm sorry. *[Beat.]* But, you know what? School is starting in just two weeks. You'll meet so many new friends. And you can go over to their house and they can come here.

BEN. But, none of them will be like Henry. He was totally ridiculous!

RORY. I bet you'll meet a best friend the first week of school.

[BEN raises HIS head and looks at HIS Dad.]

BEN. You think so?

RORY. I know so. What do you think Mom?

 KATE. Absolutely.

BEN. *[He has a new worry.]* What if Reverend Tuttle comes back? He smelled funny.

CLAIRE. We'll use our magic dust on him and make him dance and sing.

BEN. What magic dust?

CLAIRE. Oh, didn't Hank tell you. He left some with me, for just such an emergency.

BEN. Really?

CLAIRE. Yes, and this time, if Tuttle comes back, we'll make him sing something from 'My Fair Lady'. How 'bout it?

[As the lights fade, KATE starts singing 'The Rain in Spain', RORY and CLAIRE sing the opposing, 'I think she's got it', all to BEN's complete delight.]

CURTAIN

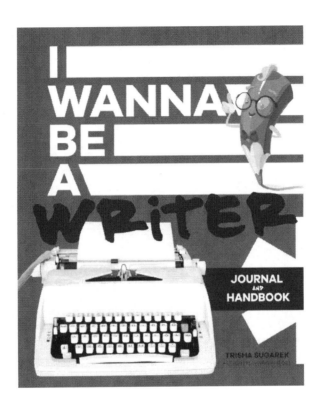

See all of Sugarek's custom Journals/Handbooks at:
https://www.amazon.com/s/ref=nb_sb_noss_1?url=search-alias%3Daps&field-
keywords=journals%2C+sugarek

And other fine book stores.

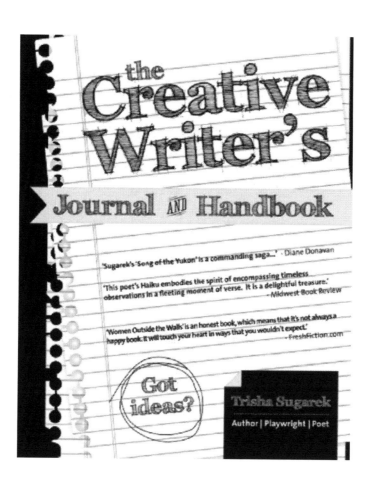

Made in the USA
Columbia, SC
13 July 2018